MARK WEBBER

MARK WEBBER

2010 - A SEASON TO REMEMBER

MACMILLAN
Pan Macmillan Australia

First published 2010 in Macmillan by Pan Macmillan Australia Pty Limited
1 Market Street, Sydney

A CIP catalogue record for this book is available from the National Library of Australia

ISBN: 9781405040037 (pbk.)

Internal design by Luke Causby, Blue Cork Pty Ltd
Typeset in DIN Regular by Luke Causby, Blue Cork Pty Ltd
Printed in Australia by Australian Book Connection

Papers used by Pan Macmillan Australia Pty Ltd are natural, recyclable
products made from wood grown in sustainable forests. The manufacturing
processes conform to the environmental regulations of the country of origin.

For all the believers out there

CONTENTS

INTRODUCTION

The world looks very different when you're lying on your back on a bush road in Tasmania with a right leg so badly broken you can't bring yourself to glance at it. That was the situation I found myself in on 22 November 2008. Was my career as a Formula 1 driver over? To tell the truth, I wasn't even thinking about racing cars. My mind was on the bigger picture: would there be damage to my legs, my spine? Was my whole way of life about to change?

Within 81 days I was back at the wheel of my Red Bull–Renault, proving my (relative) fitness to the key people at Red Bull Racing as the start of the 2009 Formula 1 World Championship season loomed. By 29 March I was able to line up on the grid for the opening round, my home race in Australia. Less than four months later, in my 130th race in F1, I became Australia's third Grand Prix winner.

For much of that intensely competitive year, I was a title contender, and while becoming Australia's third World Champion eventually had to be put on hold, I did end the year with my second Grand Prix win in Brazil and a thrilling run to second place in another Red Bull one–two finish at the new event in Abu Dhabi. So 2009 was what they call a 'breakthrough year'.

The change of fortune continued into 2010. For the first time in my F1 career I took pole position in successive races in Spain and Monaco, then completed the hat-trick in Istanbul. Barcelona brought victory number three in a Formula 1 car, and two weeks later Monte Carlo gave me the greatest day of my life – I was the first Australian to win there since the incomparable Jack Brabham, as he was then, way back in 1959.

Then came the infamous Istanbul incident when my teammate Sebastian Vettel and I crashed while heading for another Red Bull one–two, and two races later many spectators around the world held their breath when my car was catapulted off the back of Finn Heikki Kovalainen's Lotus as I went to pass him in the European Grand Prix. Ups and downs? You said it!

But if breaking my leg in Tasmania was the absolute low point, an accident that left me fighting for my sporting life, then Monaco less than 18 months later was the absolute high – so far. Throughout my career as a racing driver I have come under pressure, usually from myself, to raise the bar on my performance, both physically and mentally. There have been several turning points, times when I had to ask myself if I could go to the next level that every sporting champion must push themselves to reach. Other people have asked the same question about me. Up front is how I am with people. Up front is where every racing driver wants to be. I hadn't really been there in F1 until 2009. In 2010 I was rarely anywhere else.

2009

A SECOND AND A HALF

2009
A SECOND
AND A HALF

In the last second and a half I knew I was in trouble.

The pain was instantaneous in both legs. Dad was there with me and I said to him, 'Mate, I'm suffering ...' My left leg was bleeding heavily but I didn't have the balls even to look at my right leg because I knew it was bad. It was 22 November 2008, a date I will never forget. And yet the day had started out so well ...

It was day four of the 2008 Mark Webber Pure Tasmania Challenge. I was the fittest I'd ever been. The strings on my bow were all strong, I had a big engine and I was really enjoying it. After an 18-kilometre morning run we'd been on our bikes for 40, maybe 45 minutes. We were supposed to be on a kayaking leg but the sea was up and we'd switched. I couldn't have been happier.

Then we hit a downhill stretch on a typical Australian bush road, about one-and-a-half lanes wide rather than the full two, and that's when I first saw it: a four-wheel drive coming round the bend towards me. The windscreen was a mirror because of the forest canopy so I couldn't see the driver's eyes or hands; I had no cues to work from. In the end, I ran out of time to avoid him. My right leg was the only thing that hit the front of the car and that sent

Late January 2009: what every well-dressed Grand Prix driver should be wearing! Sessions in this special chamber were an integral part of my rehabilitation after my fall and serious injury in Tasmania in November 2008.

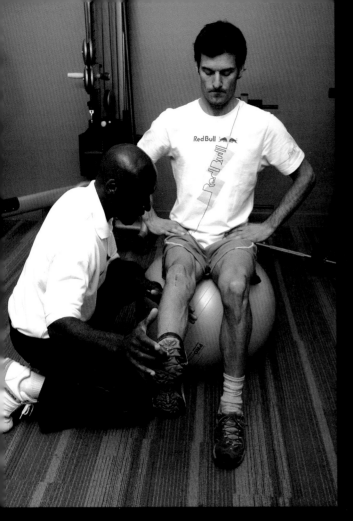

Roger Cleary put in a sensational effort to help get me ready – sort of – for the crucial first test of 2009 in Spain in February.

me spinning down the road. It was when the other competitors came past that I began to feel really bad, because they were all saying, 'It's Mark ...'

I wasn't thinking about my racing career: I was too concerned about my spine, my pelvis, life, the bigger picture. I heard one of the ambulance people – who were brilliant – saying they had to straighten my leg and get a pulse in my foot. Then the drugs started to kick in. The last thing I remember is telling the chopper pilot to fly faster.

It was just three weeks after the 2008 Formula 1 World Championship season had ended in Brazil. That had been the 121st race of my career, and while I hadn't scored points in São Paulo, I had already

reached a milestone with 100 points from my 121 Grands Prix to date. On the other hand, some pretty cluey people were already saying that the same Mark Webber was now facing the biggest challenge of his career.

My new teammate for '09 at Red Bull Racing (RBR) was the young German tipped to be the 'new Schumacher', Sebastian Vettel. A protégé of the company's junior driver training program, Seb had been in F1 for just 26 races but already he was a Grand Prix winner, a feat he accomplished from pole position for our sister team Scuderia Toro Rosso in Italy in September '08. Some insiders at RBR were confidently predicting that Seb would end my career, so the aim was to prove the doubters wrong and once again rise to the challenge as I had done throughout my racing life.

And then came the 'other' challenge in Tasmania.

The enormity of what had happened hit me four days after the accident when I got out of my hospital bed for the first time. Surgeons had inserted rods and screws to help mend the break, but I just could not believe the pressure I felt in the leg. I realised then just how long the road back to fitness was going to be. It's important to understand that preparing for a new Grand Prix season is a lengthy process and requires us drivers to front up for testing more than a month ahead of the first race. How was I going to manage that? Red Bull Racing team owner Dietrich Mateschitz had called me, and the first question he asked was, 'Mark, what are you doing? This is your event – this is not supposed to happen!' He added that they would wait for me, but it would be good if I could be ready to go testing on 9 February.

I was in no state to go anywhere – I was unable to fly for five weeks – but in my own mind I knew I was in the wrong place and it was killing me to stay at home in Queanbeyan, feeling detached from everything and everyone. The new kid on the block was scoring all the early points within the team just by virtue of being there.

Somehow I made it to the UK before Christmas. The people who looked after my rehabilitation did a wonderful job,

This is it: first day back at the office, mid-February 2009. I look pale but interesting, don't you think?

especially when I finally got back to my UK base. Roger Cleary, my physiotherapist, was incredible: he knew my career was at stake. He organised an intensive program of pool work, static bike riding and specific exercises, and he put up with me being impatient when I couldn't see any progress. But I would be lying if I told you I was really ready for my first day back at the office.

It came at the Jerez circuit in southern Spain, on 11 February 2009. I was not in great shape at all. I was in a good deal of discomfort after the top screw had been taken out of the pins they put in my leg, but I was trying to walk as well as I possibly could in front of people like our Chief Technical Officer Adrian Newey and Team Principal Christian Horner. Basically my leg was still broken and it was the metalwork that was holding it all in place. We got there, launched our new car, the RB5, and did a press day, during which I noticed Seb going around with a real spring in his step – which I couldn't have matched if I'd tried!

But then I got straight back on the horse, as they say. The RB5 was a stunning-looking thing. The way Adrian had packaged it was just unbelievable. Any driver worth his salt would have been champing at the bit to get behind the wheel. On my second run in the car, I was very quick. I managed 83 laps, which is more than any Grand Prix distance. Though I did tire quickly and the lap times fell away, that wasn't important. The relief surged through me and I struggled out of the car grinning like the Cheshire Cat. I knew then I was going to make it to the start of the season, my home

race in Melbourne. What I didn't know was that I was about to have the season of my F1 life so far ...

Not that my racing year started well; it rarely does, for some reason, in Melbourne. I trained on the Spanish island of Lanzarote the week before flying home, and got in 200 kilometres on the bike. I was feeling pretty good. The race weekend got off to a shaky start, though, when I had a driveshaft-related problem in the opening practice session, while Seb had hydraulic issues of his own. There were a few too many reliability problems, I said at the time, and they were something we needed to get on top of quickly.

In Q3, the third session of the qualifying hour, I got a bit greedy under braking at Turn 9, and ended up tenth on the grid. As for the race, mine effectively ended on the opening lap when Brazilian Rubens Barrichello's new Brawn GP car punted my

By Round 3 things were looking up: Shanghai brought me the best result of my F1 career at that stage when I came home behind Sebastian.

TRONAS
BRIDGESTONE
PETRO
Red Bull
BRIDGESTONE
CASIO
TRONAS
TRON
M. WEBBER

Sebastian Vettel and I achieved the first one-two finish for the Red Bull Racing team.

RB5 up the backside. I had to pit for a new nose, and ended up getting some mileage in at the rear of the field rather than trying to salvage anything concrete from the race. So my first point of 2009 had to wait, and when it did come in Malaysia it was only half a point. The race had begun late at five in the afternoon and finished early when typically monsoon-like rain halted proceedings after just 33 of the 56 laps. But better things were to come.

In Shanghai, Seb and I posted the first-ever one–two finish for Red Bull Racing. Again it was wet, and we had a big advantage – it was only ever going to be between us two. Though I'd have liked to be the one to score our first victory, it was my own best result in F1 to that date, and the highlight was my dice with the man who would be 2009 World Champion, Jenson Button. I got past him, lost the place again when I ran wide, but said to myself, 'Okay, I'm going to absolutely scream round him on the outside.' It was probably one of the best moves I've ever made.

After that high, Bahrain was a low. German Force India driver Adrian Sutil deliberately baulked me in qualifying because he thought I was on an out-lap at the same time as he was; I qualified 19th and was never in the hunt even for a point, never mind anything more. Barcelona helped get things back on track, though. This time I started from the third row but put in a good middle stint of the race to get past Seb and Brazilian Ferrari driver Felipe Massa. This time it was a move on former World Champion Spaniard Fernando Alonso that made my day. I knew my race was ruined if I got stuck behind him, so I risked a lot to make it work and it carried me to the podium in third spot. It was, incidentally, my 39th points-scoring finish – equalling the number set by Australia's 1980 World Champion Alan Jones.

Monaco brought another landmark when I started for the 127th time – 11 more than AJ and, more significantly, one more than the great Sir Jack Brabham, making me Australia's longest-serving Grand Prix driver in terms of races contested. But as the races came and went, I still hadn't joined those two great names on the winners' list. Turkey was another 'nearly' day when I came second, ahead of Seb, so while I wasn't winning I was doing what a lot of people said I wasn't capable of – namely giving Seb a bloody good run for his money.

My maiden Grand Prix victory should have come two weeks later at my 'other' home race, the British Grand Prix at Silverstone, a track I know like the back of my hand. I was on course for my first pole in F1 when I caught Finn Kimi Räikkönen's Ferrari on Hangar Straight. I don't know if Kimi was drinking vodka or just dreaming,

but he was going slowly, still on the racing line, and he completely compromised my entry into Stowe Corner and screwed my chance of top spot on the grid. Starting third behind Seb, who had eventually nabbed pole, I was bottled up behind Rubens for the whole first stint; even though I jumped him in the pit stops I was never in a position to threaten for the lead, so I had to be content with my third second-place finish of the season.

And then it happened.

Before the German GP at the Nürburgring I caught up with Ricky Ponting, the Aussie cricket captain, who was in the UK to lead his team in another Ashes campaign. Ricky had come over to see me in hospital in the aftermath of my accident and a friendship had developed that meant a lot to me. We had both been driven to compete on the world stage, and by the desire to test ourselves at the highest level. Over and over again we had both asked ourselves the question: 'Can I do it?' For me, the answer came on 12 July 2009 – the day I really did run up front all the way.

This was the greatest weekend of my life. It was my 130th Grand Prix, and I began it from my first F1 pole position. Coincidentally I had just come from some of my best training, on my bike in the hills near our home at Vence in the south of France. It was a critical time: I needed to take some of the wind out of Seb's sails, both in the World Championship and within the team. Qualifying was horrible. It was spitting with rain in the middle session, when it would have been very easy to get knocked out. In Q3 the top 10 got to see a dry track for the first time in quite a while, and it all came down to my last lap. Rubens got close to me, but we knew the Brawn GP cars were light on fuel whereas I was well fuelled for the race. I'd never been better placed to make the breakthrough to the top step of the podium.

And it nearly fell apart within the first few seconds.

I dwelt on the line – nothing unusual there! – which allowed Rubens to attack me. The problem was I didn't know which side he was attacking me from because I completely lost sight of him. I only found out where he was when I moved right – and hit him. It was wheel-to-wheel, and probably looked worse than it was because of the way both cars recoiled from the contact, but I had a feeling the stewards might not like what they had seen. I was actually more worried about my contact with defending World Champion Lewis Hamilton's McLaren a few seconds later because it damaged my car's bodywork.

Sure enough, on lap 10 the news came that I was under investigation, on lap 12 I learned I'd copped a drive-through penalty, and on lap 14 I took my medicine. 'It's just not meant to be,' was the thought running through my head, but then my engineer Ciaron Pilbeam came on the horn and told me he thought I could still win. In the end we got there comfortably – and were greeted by the 800-odd messages, texts and emails that flooded in after the race!

I'd been a Formula 1 driver for seven-and-a-half seasons. In that time I'd driven for four teams. I had started no fewer than 129 World Championship Grands Prix. And I had never won. Never started from pole position; never set the fastest lap in any of those 129 previous races. But Germany 2009 was the weekend where all that changed – and so did my life.

On the Saturday of that memorable German Grand Prix weekend, the ninth round of the 2009 World Championship, I claimed my first F1 pole position.

When I crossed that line I let rip with about 17 'yeses' and a few unrepeatable things …

Naturally there were a few people to be thanked, starting with this little beauty: my RB5. She was only first because she was with me in pit lane.

The person I wanted to get to most was my partner Ann, who's been with me every step of this incredible journey. We'd made it at last – together.

Of course my father was there with us as well. He looks as if he still hasn't grasped what's really happened to his son. I can't blame him – neither had I!

I was incredibly proud to see the Australian flag hoisted highest on the podium and around the paddock.

People often say I'm always good for a quote. After I crossed the line I came out with another one. It went something like, 'Yes! Yeeeeeeeees! You bewdy! Yes-yes-yes-yes-yes-yes-yes! Ha-ha! Yes ... yes-yes-yes-yes-yes!' I'm the first to admit it – it's not Shakespeare. The 'speech' was playing at full volume through the Red Bull factory the first time I walked back through the doors after my win.

Two weeks later I was on the podium again in Hungary, and this time I added my first F1 fastest race lap to the first pole and first victory I'd notched up in Germany. I went into the mid-season break having accumulated more points in the previous six races than any other driver out there, and

my confidence was at an all-time high.

After that break, my next five results were 9th, 9th, DNF, DNF and 17th and so my '09 title bid came off the rails. The new race at Valencia was the most boring I've ever taken part in; I had a first-lap tangle in Italy; I got pinged for passing Fernando Alonso on the outside of the track in Singapore then had my front left brake disc shatter; I had a crash in Suzuka practice that meant I couldn't take part in qualifying, then made three stops in the first five laps of the race: all a bit of a disaster.

By the time we went to Brazil in October it was clear Jenson Button was going to be World Champion. The fact that he clinched

No, I'm not having a slanging match with Fernando: this is Hungary, and a timing glitch meant we weren't sure who'd just taken pole position. It turned out Fernando had just pipped me, but I had the consolation of setting my first fastest race lap in F1 next day.

After the longest, wettest qualifying session in F1 history, race day in Brazil was sunny – and so was I after my second Grand Prix win.

Felipe Massa had missed the second half of the season after his horrible accident in Hungary, so it was doubly pleasing to see him wave the chequered flag for my second victory.

For the second time I was able to front the world's media as a Grand Prix winner – though I'm not sure what the question is I've just been asked!

SÃO PAULO

ANDE PRÊMIO PETROBRAS DO

21

I'm not the only one whose dad likes to be there when his son wins: Jenson and John Button celebrate the day when his world title slightly overshadowed my second victory.

Not only was Abu Dhabi my eighth podium of the year, it also meant Red Bull Racing finished it with another one-two result as a fantastic springboard into 2010.

the title at Interlagos rather overshadowed my second Grand Prix win! I qualified alongside Rubens Barrichello on the front row, then when Rubens pitted after the opening stint I fired in a series of hot laps to make the difference. By my own stop five laps later, I was in front. We controlled the race and won it comfortably, and one of the messages I received this time was from multiple MotoGP World Championship winner Valentino Rossi. 'Two is the double of one!' he told me, and the result made me believe it was possible to do it all again ... and again.

At the last race in Abu Dhabi it was Seb who was in front for Red Bull while I came out on top in a great battle with Jenson for second place. This was a defensive drive where I spent the last few laps making absolutely sure I got my braking-points spot-on, and it all worked out.

Having started 2009 with nothing on the scoreboard – no wins, no poles, no fastest laps – and a broken leg to boot, I ended it in fourth place in the Drivers' World Championship with three fastest laps, a pole and, crucially, two race wins among my eight podiums for the season. 'Can I do this?' I had asked myself so often. Now I knew the answer: yes I could, and I was looking forward to being up front as often as possible in 2010.

I think it's fair to say 2009 was the year when I came out of the F1 shadows ...

23

It may be in the middle of the desert, but that doesn't mean Bahrain lacks colour!

BAHRAIN
NO SMOKE WITHOUT FIRE?

BAHRAIN

Pole Position:
Sebastian Vettel (RBR–Renault),
1:54.101 = 198.739 km/h
[MW P6, 1:55.284]

Fastest Lap:
Fernando Alonso (Ferrari), 1:58.287
= 191.706 km/h, lap 45
[MW: 1:59.487, lap 45]

Podium:
1. Fernando Alonso (Ferrari)
2. Felipe Massa (Ferrari)
3. Lewis Hamilton (McLaren–Mercedes)
[MW P8]

Drivers' World Championship:
1. Alonso 25 points
2. Massa 18
3. Hamilton 15

8. Webber 4

Constructors' World Championship:
1. Ferrari 43 points
2. McLaren–Mercedes 21
3. Mercedes GP 18

4. RBR–Renault 16

RACE 1 >>> SAKHIR

Race Date:	14 March 2010
Circuit Name:	Bahrain International Circuit
Number of Laps:	49
Circuit Length:	6.299 km
Race Distance:	308.405 km
Lap Record:	1:58.287 – F Alonso (2010)

NO SMOKE WITHOUT FIRE?

We went into 2010 in very different shape from the way we'd started 2009. I'd had further surgery on the injured leg, but it was no longer a factor that might cloud my horizons. Much more importantly, I went into 2010 as a driver with Grand Prix victories under his belt. As I told Edd Straw of *Autosport* in mid-February, I was coming into this season less in hope, more in conviction. I wanted to build on 2009, and that meant targeting more than the two wins I'd achieved the previous season.

Uniform on, ready for another school year – but the class of 2010 met for the first time not in Australia, but in Bahrain.

The animals go in two by two, at least when the season starts. After that, it's every man for himself!

You may see a few of these shots in the early days of 2010 as I try to get familiar with the McLaren–Mercedes cars – F-duct and all – of the last two World Champions, Jenson Button and Lewis Hamilton.

The Formula 1 landscape had changed quite a bit, too. We had new teams in the line-up, though some of us were concerned about the lack of running the drivers would have had before taking to the track in the Middle East. We had some new faces, and also some old faces like Fernando Alonso's, in unfamiliar surroundings now at his new home, Ferrari. But we also had a very familiar face back among us. At the age of 41, seven-time World Champion Ferrari legend Michael Schumacher was making a Grand Prix comeback with a German national team in the form of Mercedes. 'Hats off to him' was my reaction. He was one of those people who had left their sport on a higher level than anyone else, but I didn't think he would be the driver he once was. He'd be bloody awesome, but would he have the hunger?

We also had some new regulations, the main one being that Formula 1 had banned mid-race refuelling. We would all start the race with the same heavy load of fuel, and that meant extra work for the chassis, the brakes and the tyres in the early stages of each race. Not only that, but the drivers who made it through to Q3 would have to start the race on the tyres they'd used to set their fastest qualifying lap. This posed us a conundrum. Should we use the softer 'option' compound tyre for extra grip on a one-lap burst with low fuel for grid position, or the harder 'prime' tyre for durability with that heavier initial race fuel load?

Last but not least, Seb and I had a new weapon in our hands: Adrian Newey's Red Bull–Renault RB6. There had been moves to

Qualifying always happens in a bit of a blur, and a little mistake on my last run meant I would kick-start my season from the third row – not the ideal place at a track like Sakhir.

Bahrain doesn't offer many chances to make a move on someone, especially when that someone is the reigning World Champion – which meant I spent a fair few laps looking very closely at his McLaren's gearbox!

switch to Mercedes power, but in the end we were sticking with what we knew. As usual, Adrian had opted to miss early pre-season testing to make sure his concept was as thoroughly developed as it could be before the car actually hit the track, which it did at the Jerez circuit in Spain, on 10 February. We had just 12 days' testing in all before hopping on the flight to Bahrain for the season's start on 14 March. RB6 was clearly an evolution of the car with which we'd won the last three races of 2009, and many of the new 2010 designs from other teams seemed to have copied that. Would Adrian have kept us ahead of the game? As usual, there were more questions than answers ...

The Bahrain circuit had been lengthened by just under a kilometre, with the addition of no fewer than five new corners after the original Turn 4. So we had 49 racing laps ahead of us and starting from sixth on the grid was not the ideal way to go about it. I was going great guns in Q3 until I locked up the rears on the way into Turn 16. That cost me two-tenths of a second, and pushing too hard to make it up cost me another four-tenths at Turn 19. The good news for the team was that Seb had planted his RB6 on pole. The bad news for me was that under the new rules the race would be hard unless you were starting from the front row.

I got away pretty well and was mixing it with the Mercedes boys – Michael and his German teammate Nico Rosberg – when my engine suddenly lost power. It sucked in too much oil, coughed violently and sent out a huge plume of smoke. I was the only one who didn't see it, which is probably a good

thing! I knew there was a bit of hesitation from the engine, but even though it happened twice, in Turns 1 and 4, it cleared quickly. And anyway, it was a nice way to spread the field out!

Then I settled in. Jenson Button got me at the top of the hill but I got him back with a move I was pretty happy with at the new, quickish right-hander. And then it was all about experiencing the new regulations to

The moment when some folks might have had their hearts in their mouths – me included! Happily it was just the Renault engine clearing its throat after swallowing too much oil.

Every circuit has its own special atmosphere, and those trees tell you this is unmistakably Bahrain.

It's a colourful sport, especially when those colours belong to Red Bull and an Australian's helmet.

the fullest. It hit me straight between the eyes during the race just how important qualifying was. In the old days you could recover some of your work if you had a bad qualifying or a problem in the early laps, but it turned out to be difficult around that track. All in all it was a clear reminder: come on, Mark, get your act together on Saturday ...

I spent most of the 49 laps getting well acquainted with the gearboxes of Michael, to start with, and then Jenson's McLaren. I tried absolutely everything: different lines, putting pressure on, but we're talking world-class drivers here and they simply don't make mistakes. I made just the one stop, on lap 16, to switch from the super-soft tyres I used in Q3 to the medium primes. The front right proved tricky to change and that cost me another four seconds, putting me back behind Jenson in eighth. And that's how it stayed. I was shocked at how hard it was to overtake, but in the race I felt very comfy with the car and I knew I was being massively held up by Michael. And my drink bottle didn't work for the whole race, so the car wasn't the only one who wasn't being refuelled!

Seb, meanwhile, had led the race for Red Bull until a broken spark plug, of all things, cost him a victory – something you might see once in a decade. But at least the car had shown itself to be competitive, and it was clearly capable of getting the right result. I was sure of that – and very much looking forward to the 'real' start to the season at my home race in Melbourne.

He casts a decent shadow: Fernando took first blood first time out for Ferrari.

AUSTRALIA

Pole Position:
Sebastian Vettel (RBR–Renault),
1:23.919 = 227.490 km/h
[MW front row, 1:24.035]

Fastest Lap:
Mark Webber (RBR–Renault),
1:28.358 = 216.061 km/h, lap 47

Podium:
1. Jenson Button (McLaren–Mercedes)
2. Robert Kubica (Renault)
3. Felipe Massa (Ferrari)
[MW P9]

Drivers' World Championship:
1. Alonso 37 points
2. Massa 33
3. Button 31

10. Webber 6

Constructors' World Championship:
1. Ferrari 70 points
2. McLaren–Mercedes 54
3. Mercedes GP 29

5. RBR–Renault 18

AUSTRALIA

BEES' DICKS AND FOXES IN THE HENHOUSE

Spot the missing part ...

RACE 2 >>> MELBOURNE

Race Date:	28 March 2010
Circuit Name:	Albert Park
Number of Laps:	58
Circuit Length:	5.303 km
Race Distance:	307.574 km
Lap Record:	1:24.125 – M Schumacher (2004)

BEES' DICKS AND FOXES IN THE HENHOUSE

What is it about the Australian Grand Prix? Like any driver, I'd give my right arm to win my home race, but apart from that memorable debut day back in 2002, I've never really had a sniff of glory at Albert Park. This year was no different, at least not on race day. Everything else had gone beautifully up until then, including the unusually hectic pre-race schedule of appearances and stops which is part and parcel of coming home for the first time as a Grand Prix winner. I'm the only Australian on the grid so a few things get slipped into the itinerary, like the 'Legends Lunch' I hosted at Southbank for my favourite Aussie sportspeople, including Glenn Archer, Damien Oliver, Mick Doohan and James Tomkins. It was a bit formal and we were all a little uncomfortable, but the company was sensational!

One nice thing about racing at home is there's often an award to pick up! I was particularly pleased to receive the one with Sir Jack's name on it.

If I can help a youngster like Mitch Evans get a foothold in Europe, I'll be happy to do it. Hope my Aussie supporters don't mind that he's a Kiwi ...

Speaking of fans, check out this colourful bunch!

37

F1's all about keeping an eye on the times. Robert did wonderfully well to work his way up to second place after qualifying ninth – but note the names at the top of the screen are all Red Bull.

Old friends having a chat. What do you suppose Michael was saying to Fernando?

So was the Red Bull performance in practice and qualifying. On Saturday afternoon it all came down to the final seconds of an exciting session, and I thought I'd got my first Albert Park pole until Seb somehow clung to his car through a ragged final few corners to edge me out by 0.116 of a second – or a bee's dick, as I believe I called it soon after. With a front row lockout we had every right to expect a great result, but Sunday turned out to be an incredibly frustrating day for both of us and for the team.

The rain came just before the race began, and when it did, the fox was well and truly in the henhouse and all hell broke loose. Both Red Bull cars started on the intermediate tyres, but I got too much wheel-spin and lost

Melbourne is a wonderful place to go racing. Too bad we can't always say the same about the local weather!

a place to Felipe's Ferrari, then as the rain eased and the conditions began to settle down, some wrong decisions were made both from the cockpit and from the pit wall. There was a safety car early on because of a stoush between Japanese Sauber driver Kamui Kobayashi and German Williams driver Nico Hulkenberg, and by the time the race restarted, a dry line was starting to show. Pole Robert Kubica's Renault was giving me the hurry-up but I got past Felipe again and Red Bull were running one–two.

But the turning point of the race was already upon us. Jenson was in for slick tyres straight away – and that decision won him the race. We ended up being way too conservative with our own decision: I didn't pit till the end of lap 10, which

Daniel Ricciardo is a young Aussie working his way through the Red Bull 'school'. He joined my dad and me to keep an eye on things.

Cars everywhere, as is so often the case at Turn 1 at Albert Park. That's me disappearing out of the shot as the rest sort themselves out behind.

Lewis had a big weekend on and off the track, and he and I had some fair old scraps at various times throughout the race.

meant I was out four laps longer on intermediate tyres than Jenson. Seb and I were out in front, so we had more to lose if a risky pit stop call went wrong, and I came in behind Seb because we have an understanding that the guy in the lead gets to stop first, so I lost out there as well. But the game was already up: we should have reacted to Jenson's move, because that was the beginning of the end.

We also had the car winged to start off the front row and disappear as our top gear was very aggressive, but we got out of position. Eventually I was very fast – on lap 17 I was half a second per sector quicker than anyone else – and I started to take a few risks, but it was difficult to make my overtaking moves work because as soon as

I went off the line it was pretty greasy. I had a bit of a straight-on at Turn 1 that let Felipe through, and when I attacked the Ferrari again Lewis's McLaren came at me in Turn 3. I got nerfed into the gravel, which let Fernando past as well and yours truly was now eighth.

I guess I should have been a lot calmer and settled for the points, but I was keen to get on the Melbourne podium and I felt I had a car that was capable of putting me there. I set the fastest race lap, a 1:28.358, with ten laps to go, so we had the pace. Lewis and I both changed tyres again to have another crack. We had a good dice, but when Lewis was trying to get past Fernando on lap 56 – just two from the finish – I was too close. He tried to set up a move then over-braked,

Not the best place to be: in hindsight I should have kept my cool instead of going all-out for glory after a difficult start to the race.

Not sure I've got John's full attention ...

as he is entitled to do in that situation, and came back across me; I had committed myself to the inside and I ran out of that last half-metre of space I needed. I lost downforce and couldn't stop myself hitting his right rear. In the end we had to settle for ninth and a reprimand from the stewards, which in one sense I suppose was fair but on the other, aren't we supposed to be out there to race?

Not only that, but Seb lost his chance of a win when he had a problem with his front left wheel and careered off the track at Turn 13 while he was in the lead. Two races gone, and Red Bull was fifth in the Constructors' Championship and I was down in tenth in the Drivers' points. This wasn't how it was supposed to be at this stage of the season, but as a team we live by the sword and die

Not the best day for us overall: Seb led early on but safety cars and, more importantly, an 'off' cost him the win.

by the sword. We have great days together and we have bad days together, and the Melbourne race day was, unfortunately, one of the latter.

It wasn't helped by the furore caused by a casual remark of mine that brought me some flak in the local media. Once again Mr Hamilton was involved! Lewis attracted the attention of the local constabulary when he did a bit of a burnout on his way out of the circuit on the Friday evening. His picture was all over the place for all the wrong reasons, while I copped a hammering from the press for calling Victoria a 'nanny state'. That remark was made in a private function room but, as so often happens, the audience wasn't quite as discreet as I thought. It was a bit of a relief, really, to get out of there and head for Malaysia ...

Sir Richard Branson was all smiles in '09 when he struck a last-minute deal with Brawn GP and 'his' cars won this race. It's a bit tougher with his 2010 newcomers, Virgin Racing.

JB was the man who got everything absolutely right on race day.

MALAYSIA

OUTBOARD MIRRORS
AND INSIDE JOBS

MALAYSIA

Pole Position:
Mark Webber (RBR–Renault),
1:49.327 = 182.523 km/h

Fastest Lap:
Mark Webber (RBR–Renault),
1:37.054 = 205.605 km/h, lap 53

Podium:
1. Sebastian Vettel (RBR–Renault)
2. Mark Webber (RBR–Renault)
3. Nico Rosberg (Mercedes GP)

Drivers' World Championship:
1. Massa 39 points
2. Alonso 37
3. Vettel 37
8. Webber 24

Constructors' World Championship:
1. Ferrari 76 points
2. McLaren–Mercedes 66
3. RBR–Renault 61

Race Date: 4 April 2010
Circuit Name: Sepang International Circuit
Number of Laps: 56
Circuit Length: 5.543 km
Race Distance: 310.408 km
Lap Record: 1:34.223 – JP Montoya (2004)

OUTBOARD MIRRORS AND INSIDE JOBS

Roger and his pit board were vital markers as I got through the treacherous conditions for my first pole of 2010.

Ever had a problem with a blind spot in your car as you go into a tricky corner? Try my RB6 as you head for Turn 1 at Sepang ... We run with outboard-mounted mirrors, which the experts tell us are worth up to a tenth of a second a lap in aerodynamic terms. Fair enough – but when it comes to telling you what's going on behind you, they're about as much use as an ashtray on the proverbial motorbike, and they almost single-handedly cost me a victory in the Malaysian Grand Prix.

Autograph sessions are part and parcel of every event we go to. Fernando's clearly into aerodynamics – but Ferrari weren't on target at Sepang.

Keeping the focus is essential: this is just before final qualifying.

For once Seb played second fiddle in these conditions.

I got the appropriate response!

It was all the more frustrating because we'd done a brilliant job in a very tricky qualifying session to put the RB6 car on pole. The whole hour was a bit of a knife-edge affair because of the fickle Malaysian weather, and in fact I only just squeezed through Q1, which is more than could be said for some very big names. Fernando Alonso, Felipe Massa and Lewis Hamilton all missed out, then Jenson Button blew Q2 when his McLaren aquaplaned off at Turn 6.

There had been standing water around the track all through the first two qualifying sessions. My engineer Ciaron Pilbeam and I made a big call to run the intermediate Bridgestone tyres for Q3, which had barely got under way when it was red-flagged for heavy rain. I was far from certain I'd made the right decision. I almost spun at Turn 2 on my first lap, but by the time I was into my second the dry line was starting to emerge.

We destroyed the field on that lap then put a margin of 1.3 seconds on them on our third! Apparently that's the biggest

The moment when my pole position advantage went south: Vettel gets the inside line as I look for him and Rosberg.

margin from pole-sitter to the second-fastest qualifier since Italian Giancarlo 'Fisi' Fisichella put his Renault on pole ahead of fellow Italian Jarno Trulli's Toyota in Melbourne back in 2005, although those were the days of two qualifying sessions and aggregate times. Still, my lap was pretty interesting in places – I had a bit of aquaplaning in the final corner – but I kept it on the black stuff and got the job done.

Well, actually I got half the job done.

The advantage was gone within a few seconds of the race start as we headed for the first right-hander. Seb started directly behind me on the second row. I had a look to see where he was as I was going through second and third gears and he wasn't mega-close at that stage. Nico Rosberg had put his Mercedes on the front row with me and I wasn't sure where he was either. That track is so wide it's difficult to defend at the best of times but if anything I thought Seb would go for my outside.

I only saw him when we both got on the brakes for that first corner and he was on my inside instead. As soon as I saw him there I thought, 'My God, for the whole race now I'll be in second ...' I considered having a crack at him as we went through the downhill section through Turns 2 and 3 but by now I was on the dusty side of the track and I couldn't afford to leave my braking too late, so the only other chance was the pit stops. I could have jumped Seb for the lead in the stops, but he had track position and so he pitted first on lap 23. Even a string of personal best sectors on my in-lap next time round didn't help me – and neither did a sticking wheel-gun on my front right during

my stop, which cost me something in the order of two-and-a-half seconds, so my fate was effectively sealed.

The first part of each race is crucial these days, so a touch of wheel-spin off the line and those bloody mirrors put paid to my chances, which was such a pity after our gamble had paid off so handsomely the day before. It was even more heartbreaking because Seb wasn't that quick. At times he was saying he was controlling the race, but he wasn't mega-fast. It would have been easier for me to get my head round the final result if he'd beaten me by 20 seconds, but I was basically shadowing him and he was just going through the motions, doing what he needed to do. I was very disappointed – probably one of my worst second places emotionally. It could have gone either way but in the end Seb did the job at the crucial stage and he deserved to win it.

I was on the back foot through the first sequence and we were under strict orders to keep cool.

The Lotus name was back with its new Malaysian connection, but Trulli had a tough time of it.

The things you see at the side of the track!

2

I wasn't happy about that number.

You can tell how much a podium meant to Nico Rosberg and his mates in the new-look Mercedes team.

Most of the interesting stuff for the fans went on behind us and a lot of it involved the McLaren boys, Jenson and Lewis, making their way through the field after their disastrous qualifying sessions. Lewis got away with a black-and-white flag warning for weaving to keep Russian Renault driver Vitaly Petrov at bay, but he did a pretty good job to come through from the back of the grid to finish P6. Fernando did his usual fighting job until his Ferrari's engine let him down near the end. I'm told Spaniard Jaime Alguersuari in the sister car from Toro Rosso pulled off the move of the race when he went round the outside of Nico Hulkenberg's Williams at Turn 5 and got his car into the points.

It was still a sensational result for the team, getting us right back into the picture

It was Seb's day and a great result for the team.

Heikki was thrilled to get his car into Q2 and earn a hug from team boss Tony Fernandez.

in both championships. We were able to let the engines relax a bit in the latter stages, although I did fire in the fastest lap of the race with four to go. Looking at it from the outside, some people will say it seems ridiculous that the first corner of a 56-lap race should decide the eventual result, but the fact is it's still extremely difficult to pass in F1, especially when the man you're trying to pass is your teammate in an identical front-running car. Should I have kept scrapping with Seb after the start? Well, we'd had a chat with Team Principal Christian Horner just before the race on that very subject. 'Boys, behave yourselves!' he'd said, and we'd taken the message to heart. We fight pretty hard within the team, but at that time the spirit and the chemistry were awesome. There would be moments later in the year when I couldn't really say the same.

Round 4, you might say, took us to
the wide open spaces – it was getting
back that was the problem!

CHINA
UNDER A CLOUD . . .
AND BLOWN AWAY

CHINA

Pole Position:
Sebastian Vettel (RBR–Renault),
1:34.558 = 207.529 km/h
[MW front row, 1:34.806]

Fastest Lap:
Lewis Hamilton (McLaren–Mercedes),
1:42.061 = 192.273 km/h, lap 13
[MW: 1:42.609, lap 14]

Podium:
1. Jenson Button (McLaren–Mercedes)
2. Lewis Hamilton (McLaren–Mercedes)
3. Nico Rosberg (Mercedes GP)
[MW P8]

Drivers' World Championship:
1. Button 60 points
2. Rosberg 50
3. Hamilton, Alonso 49

8. Webber 28

Constructors' World Championship:
1. McLaren–Mercedes 109 points
2. Ferrari 90
3. RBR–Renault 73

Race Date: 18 April 2010
Circuit Name: Shanghai International Circuit
Number of Laps: 56
Circuit Length: 5.451 km
Race Distance: 305.066 km
Lap Record: 1:32.238 – M Schumacher (2004)

UNDER A CLOUD ... AND BLOWN AWAY

The circuit in Shanghai is distinctive, not only because of the buildings (including the bizarre Media Centre over the track) but also because of the layout of the track itself. It's one of German architect Hermann Tilke's designs, and they tell me it's meant to look like the Chinese symbol meaning 'high'. That may be so, but the Chinese race was a low for Red Bull Racing, and we left the country under a cloud, both literally and metaphorically.

It all started well enough: Seb and I locked out the front row of the grid, as we had done in Melbourne and nearly did in Malaysia, but this time the advantage went Seb's way. We pushed each other again throughout qualifying and I was faster in Q1 and Q2. Seb later admitted that he and his engineers decided to follow in the direction of my car with their settings, and in Q3 he stopped the hourglass quicker than I did. We both did our first Q3 runs on the harder tyres to keep a set of softs for the race. I went out

All those brollies
added a bit of colour.

The boss man, Bernie Ecclestone, with the circuit that's supposed to be laid out like the Chinese symbol for 'high'.

first for my final crack and I was quickest at the time, but then I realised Seb was already going faster on his last run. The stopwatch doesn't lie, and that's how it went. I gave it everything but it wasn't enough. I would have liked to have been further up, but in the end we both got the positions we deserved.

The front row was still a good position to start, beating Fernando's Ferrari and the two McLarens, especially when you consider the build-up to this long-haul round of the Championship. That Icelandic volcano with the unpronounceable name had gone up in smoke, and most of it seemed to have settled over northern Europe. Getting gear all the way to China was a challenge – there was even stuff coming out on the Friday night that we should never have been able

to get to China at all. It wasn't easy for the team to arrange, so it was a real credit to everyone at the Milton Keynes factory.

Things didn't look too bad at race start. Fernando shot into the lead but it was clear he'd jumped the start; I managed to get ahead of Seb, so effectively we were running in another Red Bull one–two formation. Then all hell broke loose further back in the pack, and the safety car came out before the end of the opening lap when Italian Force India driver Vitantonio Liuzzi, Swiss Toro Rosso driver Sebastien Buemi and BMW Sauber's Kamui Kobayashi got tangled up. The safety car was in after six laps but by then rain became a factor so an early pit stop was on the cards ... and once again my first one was a bit of a disaster.

As I made for the pit box I locked the front tyres on the wet surface and instead of gliding to a graceful halt I skidded into the jack they use to lift the front of the car. Both car and jack were damaged so I couldn't get the full service job I wanted. I was in again after 19 laps for a new set of intermediate tyres and this time the right front played up, so the pit stops had done me no favours at all. Seb was running less wing than I was, and therefore was quite a bit faster on Shanghai's kilometre-long straight – you could see where things were heading.

A second safety car was deployed on lap 21, while I was running ninth, when the Spanish Toro Rosso driver Jaime Alguersuari and Brazilian HRT driver

Bruno Senna collided. Jenson, who by this time was controlling the race, slowed right down behind the safety car as we got ready for the restart. Everyone just began dive-bombing each other: Lewis hit me as we came through the last corner and that pushed me wide onto the astroturf. It was so wet I had to go beyond it and onto the tarmac, and by the time I got the car back on the track I'd dropped another six spots.

After that we were back to front: quick in all the wrong places, like the middle sector, when we needed that pace through the two turns before that long straight. I pitted for a last set of intermediate tyres on lap 35 but they were buggered long before the race finished. It was like a flashback to my Formula Ford days: no grip whatsoever!

Changeable weather is always a bit of a nightmare over a Grand Prix weekend. Things looked bright in qualifying ...

The tail-light shows you how quickly things could change.

Is this what snappers mean by 'red eye'? Hands up if you guessed correctly: it's Fernando keeping a close watch on his monitor in the pits.

It wasn't supposed to be this way: that's Fernando's Ferrari getting the better of us despite our front row lockout.

I never thought I'd be behind Michael when he was seeing blue flags waved!

At least there were some people who weren't happy to see the back of him!

MICHAEL

F1 WITHOUT YOU LIKE LIFE WITHOUT SEX

Who said it's not a team sport?

Mind you, it can get a bit strained when you get stacked up in pit lane …

All in all it was a tough race as the balance of the car just went away from us in the wet conditions. The bottom line is that neither Red Bull car was quick enough on the intermediate tyres. To round it all off, Seb was reprimanded, as was Lewis, for their scary side-by-side exit after the early pit stop. Our fourth straight points-scoring finish was small consolation – the big points come much further up the field than my eighth-place finish in Shanghai.

To make matters worse, the one thing that hadn't been blown away was that cloud – the real one filled with volcanic ash. We bantered about it in the post-qualifying press conference: Seb said he was renting a car to drive home on a one-stop strategy; I said I might keep

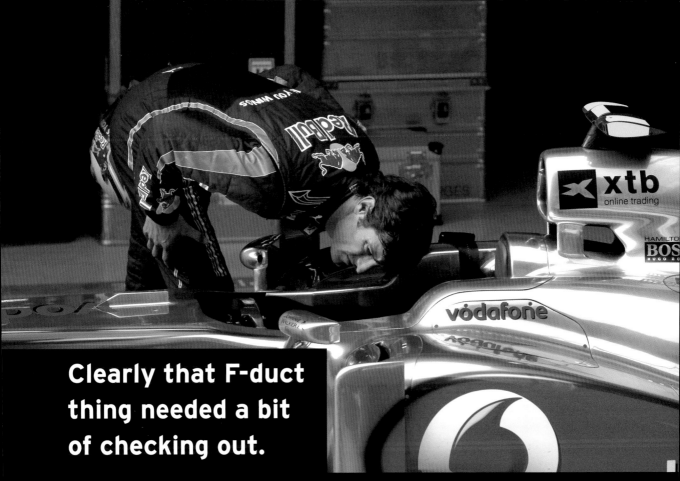

Clearly that F-duct thing needed a bit of checking out.

going the same way to end up in Australia, and Fernando suggested I should swim. In the end Christian Horner and I flew from Shanghai to Dubai on the Monday morning and from there to Rome. We switched airports in Rome and flew to Nice, spending the night there, and early on Tuesday we were on one of the first flights to go through British airspace – but we had to go to Glasgow to do it. When we got to Scotland I discovered I'd lost my passport. This was a real shame because it contained all my racing history – it was one of those monster passports, and there were only two pages left. By the time we got the final leg over and done with – a chopper transfer to Oxfordshire – we'd completed a five-stop strategy and a two-day race! Meanwhile Seb got a lift with

F1 supremo Bernie Ecclestone to Istanbul, took a flight to Nice and then drove home – a one-stopper as he had promised – but the bulk of the team and the cars didn't make it home till the Thursday.

It was the Button household that had cause for celebration in China.

Happy anniversary, Catalunya: this was the 20th time the circuit had staged a World Championship Grand Prix and of course we just had to break the diet.

SPAIN
¡Olé!

SPAIN

Pole Position:
Mark Webber (RBR–Renault),
1:19.995 = 209.488 km/h

Fastest Lap:
Lewis Hamilton (McLaren–Mercedes),
1:24.357 = 198.655 km/h, lap 59
[MW: 1:24.828, lap 62]

Podium:
1. Mark Webber (RBR–Renault)
2. Fernando Alonso (Ferrari)
3. Sebastian Vettel (RBR–Renault)

Drivers' World Championship:
1. Button 70 points
2. Alonso 67
3. Vettel 60
4. Webber 53

Constructors' World Championship:
1. McLaren–Mercedes 119 points
2. Ferrari 116
3. RBR–Renault 113

RACE 5 >>> CATALUNYA

Race Date: 9 May 2010
Circuit Name: Circuit de Catalunya
Number of Laps: 66
Circuit Length: 4.655 km
Race Distance: 307.104 km
Lap Record: 1:21.670 – K Räikkönen (2008)

¡OLÉ!

Familiarity breeds contempt, the saying goes, and there is no track on the World Championship calendar that F1 drivers are more familiar with than the Circuit de Catalunya at Montmeló, to the north of Barcelona. In 2010 the circuit celebrated its 20th anniversary as a Grand Prix venue. For many of those years we have been going there to perform thousands of laps in testing, not to mention our annual visit for the Spanish Grand Prix itself. It's not really a question of contempt, of course, because it's a superb venue, but it's fair to say that sometimes we all get a little tired of it. So what happened on the weekend of 8 and 9 May 2010 gave me a whole new perspective on the place.

The 2010 season had kicked off less spectacularly than I had hoped. Okay, I'd been on the front row everywhere except Bahrain, but apart from our one–two finish in Malaysia I hadn't been on the podium. By this time I was back in eighth place in the Championship; Jenson was leading on 60 points after those wins in Australia and China, and his score was twice mine. While the new points allocation for 2010 meant there was no cause for panic (you get 25 for a win), it was definitely time to start putting some serious runs on the board. Barcelona was where the fight-back began.

Our RB6 was fourth, second and second in the three practice sessions, so we knew we were looking good, but just before qualifying began, Christian made a telling comment. 'You probably won't get to drive a car like this around here too often,' he said, 'so go and enjoy it.' If you've kept half an

No, your eyes are not deceiving you: before going to Barcelona I went to Italy for a promotional outing. 'See Naples and ... fly?'

Still haven't got there: we're in Britain to celebrate the opening of the 'new' Silverstone with Scot David 'DC' Coulthard, Damon Hill and the Duke of York. It would turn out to be a happy omen ...

Now we're in Spain, and as you can see we occasionally do something useful, such as helping out excellent causes like the 'Wings for Life' charity.

eye on my career, you'll know that I've been in plenty of F1 cars that really weren't all that good, so I took his message to heart.

It was a sensational qualifying session. When you can stay flat in sixth gear through Turn 9 at Catalunya you know your backside is in a pretty special machine. No wonder Lewis said our cars were 'ridiculously fast'! The Red Bulls were quickest in each of the three sessions, with me just pipping Seb each time. In Q3 the RB6 was the only one to break the 1:20 minute barrier, so Red Bull were on pole for the second race in a row. Seb has a great record against me in qualifying, I can't deny that, but if you look closely you will see that the numbers are always very, very tight and it was nice to

Bewdy! We were back on pole in Barcelona.

I wasn't the only one who was happy to be there!

Adrian, meanwhile, was treating himself to a look at some of his rivals' work before the race got under way.

'Brake late and see what happens' – and it worked as this time I got the inside running and kept the advantage pole had given me.

I had the whip hand as we settled into the first lap.

have another one go my way. In the post-qualifying press conference I made a point of saying that the back-to-back races in Spain and Monaco could have a big bearing on things and it was good to have laid such a solid foundation for the week's work ahead.

Sitting on pole in Catalunya you have plenty of time to contemplate that long run down to the first corner. 'Brake late and see what happens' was my highly technical approach – and it worked. I got away beautifully, went inside – no repeat of the Malaysian cock-up – and held position through the corner. I was never headed after that, and this time even my one and only pit stop went perfectly when I came in on lap 17 to switch to the prime tyres.

By that time the main threat was not the other Red Bull car but Lewis, who had

jumped Seb at the pit stops. The addition of the F-duct gave Lewis's McLaren a speed advantage on the straights so it had pretty decent pace. It was just a matter of keeping an eye on him and putting the hammer down when he got caught in slower traffic. In the end he went off at Turn 3 and my last two laps were untroubled. But it still felt like the longest Grand Prix I've ever done: it was all about watching the lap board count down and it seemed to take forever to get to 66!

It was amazing to think we'd put in a dominant performance like this on the back of that epic Shanghai journey. A lot of people were inconvenienced by the disrupted flights, so it speaks volumes for the intensity of the guys and the team's ability to push so hard that we achieved

This was a day when the bad luck went our main rivals' way – as with Lewis's wrecked McLaren.

It didn't do Karun Chandhok much good that his team was called Hispania or his car carried a bit of the local lingo ...

That was Fernando behind me in the champagne mist: his performance thrilled both him and his home fans first time out there in a Ferrari.

The guys had buried themselves to get our cars race-ready after the travel chaos on the way back from Shanghai, so it was only right that chief mechanic Kenny Handkammer should come up there with us to celebrate a brilliant one–two result.

It was a great feeling to be
spraying the champagne again
for the first time since Brazil '09.

this victory. Especially when there were wholesale changes to almost every one of the car's surfaces before it rolled out of the garage. With Jenson handicapped by a dash read-out failure on his McLaren and Seb also in difficulties with his brakes, they didn't earn many points so the win saw me go from eighth to fourth in the points standings. Seb's third place meant Red Bull had taken a chunk out of the front-runners in the Constructors' table as well.

Such a special day called for an equally special celebration. I had made a promise over the winter that when I won a Grand Prix in 2010 I would try to do something a little bit different. MotoGP champion Jorge Lorenzo was at the race but I wasn't about to try to copy his two-wheeled victory antics! When I climbed out of my car at the end of

the race the crowd opposite the pits was going mad – probably something to do with a Spanish bloke called Alonso finishing second in a Ferrari! There wasn't much prospect of a proper celebration that evening since we had to report for duty in Monaco by the following Wednesday, so it seemed natural that I should sprint across the track and lob my helmet into the crowd. It was my way of saying thanks to them all – the Alonso followers included – for their support of our sport. In fact, the helmet turned up again later. The youngster who caught it contacted a Spanish TV station to see if they could get it signed, and they brought it to one of the races where we did a piece for the young lad on camera. So it wasn't such a bad thing that it had ended up in the middle of a bunch of Ferrari fans!

Jorge Lorenzo was a high-profile visitor to the race, but I wasn't about to copy one of his crazy winning celebrations!

Still, a special day did call for a special gesture ...

Too bad there were no Aussies in the front row!

73

MONACO

Pole Position:
Mark Webber (RBR–Renault),
1:13.826 = 162.869 km/h

Fastest Lap:
Sebastian Vettel (RBR–Renault),
1:15.192 = 159.910 km/h, lap 71
[MW: 1:15.318, lap 63]

Podium:
1. Mark Webber (RBR–Renault)
2. Sebastian Vettel (RBR–Renault)
3. Robert Kubica (Renault)

Drivers' World Championship:
1. Webber 78 points
2. Vettel 78
3. Alonso 75

Constructors' World Championship:
1. RBR–Renault 156 points
2. Ferrari 136
3. McLaren–Mercedes 129

Not your usual pit lane setting, is it?
It might not get the thumbs-up from
a modern track selection panel but
Monaco remains the jewel in F1's crown.

MONACO
THE GREATEST DAY

RACE 6 >>> MONTE CARLO

Race Date: 16 May 2010
Circuit Name: Circuit de Monaco
Number of Laps: 78
Circuit Length: 3.340 km
Race Distance: 260.520 km
Lap Record: 1:14.439 – M Schumacher (2004)

THE
GREATEST
DAY

Formula 1 is a world of contrasts – none bigger than the one between the Circuit de Catalunya and the streets of Monaco. Going from Barcelona, where my pole-winning lap averaged almost 210 km/h, to Monte Carlo, was like taking a giant step back in time. People say that if you wanted to introduce Monaco to the race calendar today they'd laugh you out of court, but it remains what it has always been: the Blue Riband event, the one every driver in his heart of hearts would love to win.

I had already done it – but not in a Formula 1 car. Back in my Formula 3000 days the place almost destroyed me. It was a hot day in early June 2000. I had forgotten to put a drink bottle in the car and with 15 laps to go I was suffering. I was so dehydrated I was almost hallucinating and was in fourth place when I crashed heavily. 'Bloody hell,' I thought, 'how do those F1 blokes do 78 laps around here? And how can I expect to do it if I can't last 50 in an F3000 car?' Well, I went back with Super

76

GENES

3.5m MENTON

arvotto
ges

MONTE CARLO
Casino

Casino

QUAI ANTOINE 1er

aldi Forum

H Monte-Carlo Beach ★★★★
O Méridien Beach Plaza ★★★★
T Monte-Carlo Bay & Resort ★★★★
E
L
S Port Palace ★★★★ L

GP
GRAND PRIX DE MONACO
FORMULA ONE
PADDOCK

H
O Miramar ★★★
T
E
L
S Fairmont Monte Carlo ★★★★ L

RMETURE à la CIRCULATION
Av. J.F. KENNEDY
0 AVRIL à 14h au DIMANCHE 2 MAI à
DI 12 MAI à 14h au DIMANCHE 16 MAI à 20h

De Paris ★★★★ L H
Hermitage ★★★★ L T
Métropole Palace ★★★★ L E
Galerie Commerciale S

This could get confusing at 160-odd
kilometres an hour! It's at Ste Dévote
– and we head left up the hill.

RENAULT

RENAULT

TW STEEL

B

TOTAL

TW STEEL

Trinasolar MOVIT

RENAULT

More than anywhere, Monaco is about track position:
Robert Kubica knows that and did everything he could
to plant his Renault on pole, but we just got there.

77

Nova Racing the next year and I was ready. 'I'm in charge this season, not you,' I told Monaco, 'and this time I'm going to rip you apart.' And in May 2001 I did: pole position, fastest race lap and victory.

But that was then, this was now, and we didn't have the best of practice sessions on the Thursday – we always start a day early in Monaco – because we did limited running and I didn't feel comfortable with what was going on. On Saturday morning we made some changes and bang: we knew we were in the hunt. It felt like I found another gear in terms of confidence in the car, and at Monaco, where you need to be so accurate and you're constantly putting everything on the line, that trust in yourself and in the car is what makes all the difference.

Here, more than at any other circuit we race on, track position is crucial because it is so difficult to overtake. I don't view Monaco as racing against other people; at Monaco it's you against the track. The track is always trying to beat you, suck you in: sometimes you get away with some small errors, sometimes you make a small error and you've got no corners on your car. So getting pole for the second straight race was a brilliant result. I told my engineer Ciaron Pilbeam laps 3 and 4 were the ones I was going to try to murder if I could. The first one was okay: I brushed the Armco barrier pretty hard at the start of the second sector, but I got the lap finished and went for another, just to tidy up the details, and it all came together. For a moment it looked as if Robert Kubica's Renault might

Here's a bloke who'd been there several times before – and seemed pretty impressed by what we'd done this time.

The best seat in the house: I've got past the little hiccup on the start line and I'm safely away in the lead as we go through Ste Dévote and up towards Casino Square.

Our Championship position got a big boost not only from another Red Bull one-two but also when key rivals like Jenson were out of the running early in the race.

One for the album: it's not often an Aussie has led and won the race that bears this name.

I thought two of these were bad enough back in '01 – this time I had four to contend with, but that's Monaco for you.

spoil the party, but in the end we'd done enough and that was a huge boost for race day. Just to show how unforgiving Monaco is, Fernando had put his Ferrari in the barriers at the long left-hander known as Massenet, damaging the chassis, and the rules state you can't use two on the same day, so the Ferrari was out of qualifying altogether.

For a fleeting moment as the race started I thought I'd thrown it all away. I didn't know if it was my fault, or whether the guys hadn't set the clutch right, but I got away with it and that was my only alarm of the day. Back in '01 I'd had two safety car periods to contend with; this time there were four! The first came early on when Nico Hulkenberg lost his Williams in the tunnel, but I was seven-tenths quicker than anyone on the first flying lap after the restart. Then Rubens

lost the other Williams going up the hill towards the casino but I got away well after that restart, too. There was a third safety car deployed when stewards spotted a loose drain cover. The only real scare was right at the end when Jarno Trulli's Lotus and Karun Chandhok's Hispania got in a fight. I was coming up behind Jarno when I saw him make a lunge down the inside at the La Rascasse corner, the tight 180-degree right-hander, in order to pass Chandhok. They interlocked wheels and all I could do was hold my breath and hope I had some options to go on the inside – and luckily enough, I did. I was home free, and the day was made even better by the fact that Seb had got in front of Robert Kubica to make it another one-two finish for Red Bull.

With that result I became the first Australian to win the Monaco Grand Prix

Well, wouldn't you be happy if you'd just come out on top after 78 laps round this place? Monaco threw everything at us but we had the answers.

Winning meant I met royalty of both kinds on the podium: the real one, in the shape of Prince Albert, and F1 aristocrat Sir Jackie Stewart!

When I jumped on the podium with the trophy, I banged it against the steel beam above the balcony! It's got a dint in the top now. I know, it's no way to treat a magnificent trophy ...

It's a long way to go for a swim, but it seemed like the right thing to do at the time!

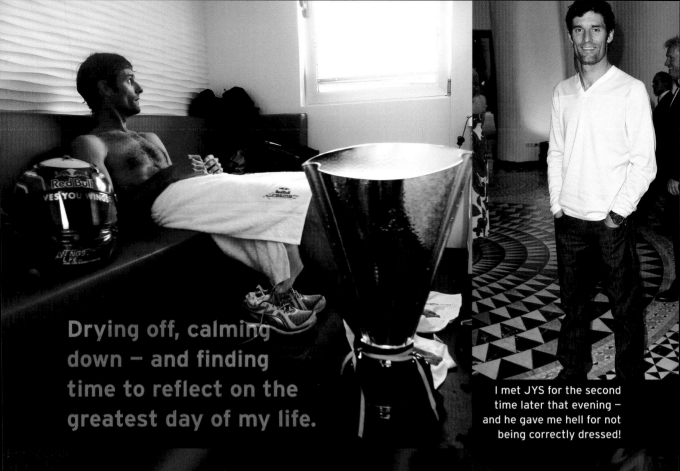

Drying off, calming down – and finding time to reflect on the greatest day of my life.

I met JYS for the second time later that evening – and he gave me hell for not being correctly dressed!

since Sir Jack Brabham back in 1959. That was the day when the rear-engined revolution really began to take hold of Grand Prix racing, and a whole new world of F1 performance opened up. In 1959, the great English driver Sir Stirling Moss was on pole with a time of 1:39.6 minutes; my time was 1:13.826. The fastest race lap went to Brabham at an average of 112.771 km/h; Seb's in 2010 was 159.910 km/h. A world of difference, brought together by two Australian drivers after more than half a century.

Except for the little hesitation at the start, we'd had an absolutely faultless day. And unlike at Barcelona, we had time to celebrate properly. I said in the post-race press conference that it might be a dangerous night for the Red Bull crew,

and it began with impromptu leaps into the little swimming pool on top of our paddock facility. Later I was one of the guests of honour at the royal palace. Naturally I didn't have a suit to wear, so it was the usual Webber jeans and casual top. Just my luck: another of the knights of motor racing, Sir Jackie Stewart – a three-time winner of the Monaco Grand Prix – was on my table and he gave me hell! It was a small price to pay at the end of the greatest day of my life. As a Formula 1 driver you really hope to win races but if there were any choice in the matter then the prestigious Monaco event is the one that any driver would pick. To join legends like Ayrton Senna, Jackie Stewart and our own Sir Jack was a very, very special thing.

TURKEY
FRIENDLY FIRE

Every picture tells a story. After the infamous
'Istanbul incident' I was able to keep going and
salvage a podium finish, while Seb had to retire.
After this, things went downhill between us.

TURKEY

Pole Position:
Mark Webber (RBR–Renault),
1:26.295 = 222.687 km/h

Fastest Lap:
Vitaly Petrov (Renault),
1:29.165 = 215.519 km/h, lap 57
[MW: 1:29.195, lap 54]

Podium:
1. Lewis Hamilton (McLaren–Mercedes)
2. Jenson Button (McLaren–Mercedes)
3. Mark Webber (RBR–Renault)

Drivers' World Championship:
1. Webber 93 points
2. Button 88
3. Hamilton 84

Constructors' World Championship:
1. McLaren–Mercedes 172 points
2. RBR–Renault 171
3. Ferrari 146

RACE 7 >>> ISTANBUL

Race Date: 30 May 2010
Circuit Name: Istanbul Motor Park
Number of Laps: 58
Circuit Length: 5.338 km
Race Distance: 309.396 km
Lap Record: 1:24.770 – JP Montoya (2005)

FRIENDLY FIRE

By the time we headed for Turkey the media were having a field day. Apparently, I was off to Ferrari, or at least in the frame for a drive there in 2011. But, in truth, in Barcelona we'd pretty much agreed that I would be staying with Red Bull. Ann joked it was us who started the rumour about Ferrari in the first place! I think they flew a kite themselves just to keep Felipe Massa's demands in check.

I had told Ann and my family before Christmas that this might be my last year in Formula 1, but Red Bull were keen to keep me. I had a few interesting chats with Flavio Briatore and Bruno Michel, too. We sensed that if I kept performing well, we'd have some

tricky things to manage within the team: like how we were to deal with me matching and beating 'their boy', which clearly wasn't part of the plan. The really big question was, could I make it three victories in a row? This would have been a great thing to do, particularly up against such top competition. Occasionally, some of the media speculation is correct and sometimes it's way over the top, but this time they were uncannily accurate about the tension within Red Bull.

I went into qualifying on the back foot after an engine problem on Friday and a difficult practice session on Saturday morning. But I knew I could dig deep and get something out of it. In the end I got

lucky: Seb had a broken roll-bar in Q3 which certainly cost him a front row spot if not better, so I picked up pole.

In the first part of the race, Lewis was very strong on the option tyres and was all over me. The two of us managed to open up a gap on Seb and because I had that little bit of daylight, the team could pit me first, cover Lewis and still get me out in front. This helped Seb a lot because then he managed to jump Lewis when he pitted.

Heading into the latter part of the race, I was the first of the front-runners to catch the back-markers. They're not exactly rocket ships, those Hispania racing things, so you've got to watch carefully what part of the

track you pass them on. On that particular lap, Karun Chandhok didn't behave amazingly well, which meant Seb was now gaining. Not only that, we'd turned my engine down a bit. Whenever we had done that in the past, we didn't fight each other, so I was asking what Seb's position was in terms of his engine. I don't think Ciaron was fully aware of what was happening: I was asking for certain information, Ciaron was struggling to get that information ...

Going into Turn 12, Seb had a top-speed advantage and I gave him room to come down the inside. Suddenly we were side by side, then he swung right and we collided. There was no malice in the 'incident' at all, and as it happened so quickly, it's not like we had half an hour to chew it over.

For some, that would've been the worst day of their lives but I've had worse. It was unfortunate and straight away I felt for everyone at the factory and also Red Bull owner Dietrich Mateschitz. I did think things were getting out of hand, but I did an extra lap and got the car back to the pits. The front wing was destroyed but we had a good lead over Michael so were able to get home in third while Seb was stuck in the gravel and making strange gestures as he walked back to the garage. In the end, there was a bit of friendly fire and I was lucky to come out of it better than Seb. But the way the press

reacted you'd have thought we'd started World War III.

It was an entirely new situation for Red Bull Racing. I tried to use my experience as best I could under the circumstances, and my point of view now is the same as it was four minutes after the race. I went from the cockpit to the podium into one of the fullest press rooms I've seen – they were baying for blood. Then, to be frank, the team was caught off guard. People were ill-informed, people made comments which had personal, emotional attachments. You know the saying someone who's had five beers says things they shouldn't? Well, that's what happened in Turkey.

The weekend began shakily when I had an engine failure in the second free practice session and then hydraulic problems in the last session before qualifying on Saturday.

If you think that's a slightly quizzical look, you're right: pole position – my third in a row – was an unexpected bonus after Seb had a roll-bar problem in Q3.

Things went pretty well early on as Lewis and I opened up a handy gap on Seb, but the action heated up when my teammate got past the McLaren in the pit stops.

It was back to serious business after the incident when I pitted to replace that second-hand front wing and rejoin the race before Michael came by.

I got off relatively lightly: Seb was going nowhere now.

Check out the media scrum waiting for Seb when he got back to the garage!

That silverware should have been in the Milton Keynes trophy cabinet.

91

It was no wonder our crew looked so deflated. We're racing not just for them but for about 600 people back at base as well.

It was just a car race, we touched and that can happen. But we all move on, and it's important to keep things in perspective. I guess it's easy for me to sit here and say that because I wasn't in Seb's shoes. If he had continued and I had retired I don't know how I would have responded.

As for Seb and I? Clearly our relationship changed that day. Michael had asked Seb on the parade lap, 'How do you get on with Mark?' and he'd said, 'Very well', which was true. But this incident marked the beginning of a building tension within the team. I think it's inevitable when you're teammates for a few years and you're fighting for the front spot on the grid. Lotus drivers Jarno Trulli and Heikki Kovalainen get on like a house on fire but that's because they're squabbling over 21st place. Are the McLaren boys Jenson and Lewis still going to be bosom buddies if they're still teammates in four years? I don't think so ...

To cap it all off someone had the bright idea of issuing a press release with the succinct heading 'Shit happens' along with that photo of Seb and me shrugging and smiling at each other. It was a soft attempt to prove we were still getting on which clearly we weren't because we had to be told to stand closer! The team was just trying to smooth things over which I suppose you can put down to inexperience. Perhaps it was meant as a message to the people within our team, because we drive for 600 people, but to me it was all Tom and Jerry stuff. It was also, by the way, the day that man snapped and went on the rampage with his rifle up in Cumbria, north-western England, killing 12 people. Just to put it all into perspective ...

I prefer to remember that we came out of a difficult day with another podium, and for a change Ann and I stayed on in Turkey instead of flying straight home. Normally we're stuck at the track, a long way out of the city on the Asian side, but she insisted that we head into Istanbul itself, and she was right. It's an astonishing place, and we had a lovely dinner with friends we'd met on holiday, then a lazy breakfast the next morning before flying back to get on with life.

It could only be Turkey, bridging the gap between East and West.

Who's Tom, who's Jerry? I'll let you decide ...

93

CANADA

No F-duct, no straight-line speed
– and no chance of fighting off the
really quick boys this weekend.

CANADA

OUTGUNNED FOR ONCE

RACE 8 >>> MONTREAL

Race Date: 13 June 2010
Circuit Name: Circuit Gilles-Villeneuve
Number of Laps: 70
Circuit Length: 4.361 km
Race Distance: 305.270 km
Lap Record: 1:13.622 – R Barrichello (2004)

OUTGUNNED
FOR ONCE

Anyone who knows me knows that I love the great outdoors, and it doesn't get much greater than the North American Rockies. We don't often have friends along for race weekends, but I was delighted to head across the Atlantic early to Colorado to go on a cycling camp with a few Texan mates before the Canadian Grand Prix. I also got to spend some time with another good friend, Anthony Edwards (you may know him better from *ER* or as 'Goose', Tom Cruise's buddy in the movie *Top Gun*). Unfortunately, we weren't top guns in Canada this year but there were plenty of reasons for that.

I qualified on the front row, but for the first time in 2010 a Red Bull wasn't on pole:

This is probably the kind of shot that got those Ferrari rumours started – though it looks as if I'm closing my ears to Team Principal Stefano Domenicali!

No, I'm not turning my back on Seb after 'the incident' in the previous race: I'm just sharing a joke with our Scuderia Toro Rosso colleagues at the Montreal autograph session.

These conversations are far more regular and important: that's me with my engineer Ciaron Pilbeam.

Just checking: tyres were the hot topic in the Montreal paddock, and I took a close look immediately after qualifying.

Lewis got there by a gnat's eyebrow on a different compound tyre. The whole weekend was about tyres and how they adapted to the 'new' Montreal track. Large sections had been resurfaced with a particularly fine-grain tarmac, and heavy rain on Friday meant the surface didn't 'rubber in' at all. Add to that the fact that Bridgestone's compounds were two steps apart – super-soft to medium – and you had all the ingredients for a bit of head-scratching. It seems McLaren scratched harder and deeper and came up with the right answer.

Still, we thought we could do a good job with the harder tyre, and we did. On the Saturday afternoon Lewis ran the super-soft

tyres but we went with the mediums because we thought the others were going to fall apart when it came to the race. In the end it turned out *all* the tyres fell apart.

Unfortunately, the guys found some little particles of metal in the gearbox oil of my car after the qualifying session and we decided to take our medicine and change the box as a precaution. Consequently, I copped a five-place grid penalty and started the race from P7.

This was the stage of the season when the debate over the F-duct was raging up and down pit lane. The F-duct works by having the driver manually alter the airflow onto the car's rear wing by stalling and opening a small duct in the cockpit. It's bloody prehistoric, isn't it? But it's powerful, and if you can achieve a more efficient drag on the rear wing, the car is going to be faster. And a tenth of a second gain on each straight is money for jam.

We had tried to race with the F-duct in Turkey but took it off on the Friday night and ran without it in Canada. The RB6 wasn't designed for it, whereas McLaren had built their car around it and done a great job. Their lead time was good, and fair play to them. Formula 1 is a prototype category in motorsport and McLaren pioneered this new technology. Having time to perfect a new development is really helpful when you're trying to package something as demanding as an F-duct, where there are changes from the front to the rear of the car.

The F-duct works best when you get onto it immediately coming out of a slow-speed corner, so you need pretty close

Not sure what I was saying to Lewis,
but he seemed to enjoy the joke ...

McLaren boss Ron Dennis certainly
enjoyed seeing his man take pole!

It's important to avoid the usual Canadian lap 1 carnage.

access. We had to work out how we'd use it in the cockpit; what type of glove we'd use; the position of the 'snorkel', and so on. This was a challenge mid-season – we usually spend ages testing this sort of stuff in the wind tunnel at Milton Keynes, and analysing the aerodynamic efficiency using CFD (Computational Fluid Dynamics). In the end, the guys did something a bit more 'agricultural' than Adrian would have liked, 'plumbing' the system in, and it made the car heavier. We're talking a kilo here and there but that's massive when you're usually trying to take weight out of the car.

F-duct or no F-duct, Canada turned out to be the first race since China where I didn't finish on the podium. I passed Jenson early on for third place, and pitted sooner than

Michael looks good here, but he had a difficult day in Montreal.

There was no stopping Lewis on the day – but check out that front left tyre.

What goes on the four corners can often dictate what happens in the race ...

We shouldn't forget the 'other' Seb – Sebastien Buemi from our sister team, Scuderia Toro Rosso. He briefly led during the pit stops in Canada.

I would have liked – after 13 laps (of 70!) – because the first few laps had taken their predictable toll on the tyres. I put on more Bridgestone medium compounds and was in the lead at about one-third race distance, maintaining the gap in front of Lewis. But we knew I had to go long in the middle stint in order to cut down the number of laps at the end on the super-soft tyre. I tried to keep my pace constant, but ultimately the tyres didn't like it and they just went away from me. I couldn't create the gap I needed to protect myself, and after my second stop on lap 50, I rejoined in fifth place with little prospect of getting any further forward. We decided to turn the car down and save it for Valencia.

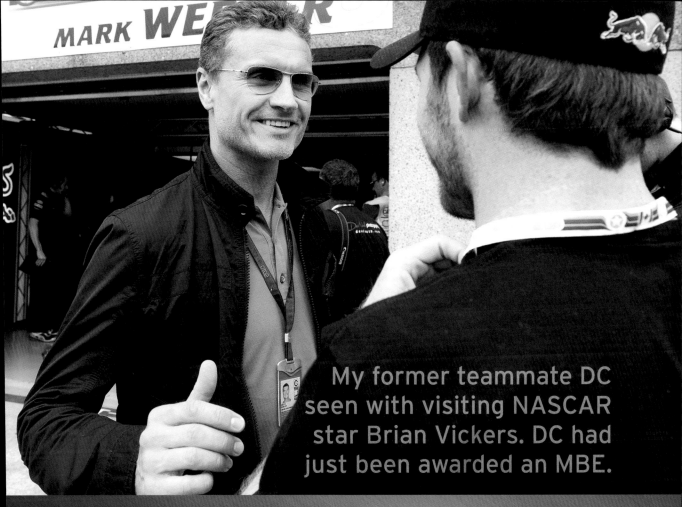

My former teammate DC seen with visiting NASCAR star Brian Vickers. DC had just been awarded an MBE.

There were some fast boys around the top five and the two McLarens and Fernando Alonso made up the podium ahead of both Red Bulls. Some felt Fernando lost the win after he struck traffic with Jarno Trulli. We expected Montreal to be a tough event and we weren't wrong. But we were more competitive than we thought, and coming home fourth and fifth was a really solid finish. It also meant I was now the only driver who had finished every race of the 2010 season in the points. There was a very interesting story in the back part of the race, but I'm going to save that for the next book!

And the F-duct? Banned for the 2011 season.

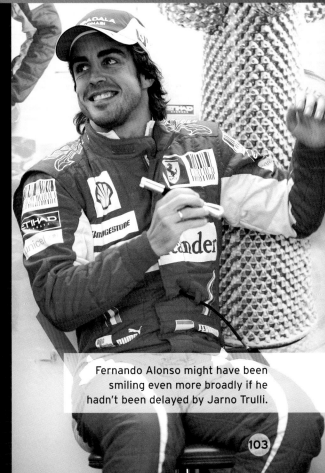

Fernando Alonso might have been smiling even more broadly if he hadn't been delayed by Jarno Trulli.

EUROPE

LOTUS GIVES
YOU WINGS . . .

Bit of a car park is Valencia, but it does
have its more interesting angles.

EUROPE

Pole Position:
Sebastian Vettel (RBR–Renault),
1:37.587 = 199.907 km/h
[MW front row, 1:37.662]

Fastest Lap:
Jenson Button (McLaren–Mercedes),
1:38.766 = 197.521 km/h, lap 54
[MW: 1:44.064, lap 5]

Podium:
1. Sebastian Vettel (RBR–Renault)
2. Lewis Hamilton (McLaren–Mercedes)
3. Jenson Button (McLaren–Mercedes)

Drivers' World Championship:
1. Hamilton 127 points
2. Button 121
3. Vettel 115

4. Webber 103

Constructors' World Championship:
1. McLaren–Mercedes 248 points
2. RBR–Renault 218
3. Ferrari 165

Race Date: 27 June 2010
Circuit Name: Valencia Street Circuit
Number of Laps: 57
Circuit Length: 5.419 km
Race Distance: 308.883 km
Lap Record: 1:38.683 – T Glock (2009)

LOTUS GIVES YOU WINGS ... ○ ○ ○

The Valencia Street Circuit on Spain's east coast is like a supermarket car park, but I haven't come away with any worthwhile purchases yet! In fact, I haven't scored a single point there since the race was incorporated into the F1 calendar two years ago. Throughout my career I've had these micro-battles with various circuits around the world and I don't intend to let them win. At the moment, Valencia has the upper hand. I'll need to take care of that next year.

Valencia is a good track for Seb and he was quick in qualifying, eventually taking pole. I went as well as I probably could have, but missed pole by a whisker and ended up with P2. The start of the race wasn't great: I was on the outside for both of the early chicanes, had a messy first sector with poor rhythm, and got beaten up – making contact with Robert Kubica's Renault. Before I knew it, I was back in eighth. It was a really tough first lap – similar to how Fernando's would be in Silverstone – and it's amazing how a race can change in just one sector.

I was fighting my way through the field but was getting held up in traffic. I started thinking that we needed to do something

Happy moment at the usual pre-weekend media call with the British guys.

a bit different ... Well, with the benefit of hindsight, it would have been better to settle for seventh or eighth place, but we were looking for more than that. I made a call on the pit stops, which was all right, then Ciaron phoned me up on the out-lap and said, 'You've got to get past Kovalainen as quickly as possible.' Of course I knew that; Ciaron was just reinforcing how important these next few laps were going to be. The Williams team had already reacted to my

The car's not the only one that has to run on a full fuel load!

Just after the start, and already I'm in trouble on the outside there, with Robert Kubica's Renault just behind and to the right of me.

You can see how narrow the track is from this view – the one I had as I came up behind Heikki ...

stop and they had their boys in the pit lane because they knew I was going to jump them if they didn't.

So I came up behind Heikki, who was moving around a little bit on the straight, and thought to myself, 'He's not going to put up much of a fight – we've got an hour and a half to go in the race, we're absolutely nowhere, he hasn't got a clue what little battle I'm involved in, he assumes I'm having a different day ...' Maybe he reckoned he could hold me up for an hour and a half but it wasn't going to happen. I got the tow in his slipstream and moved across, thinking he was letting me through, and then it all happened really fast: he braked early, I hit the back of him and at 300 kilometres per hour I didn't need Red Bull to give me wings, I just took flight!

What's bizarre in these situations – and I've been there before in the Le Mans car – is that everything goes really quiet. I remember being worried about the bridge, because I knew there was one on the track somewhere, and if you come into contact with that ... well, it doesn't bear thinking about. I was also worried about Annie, because I knew she'd be watching. But I really wasn't worried about myself. My final thought was, 'This could go either way ...'

In the end the car held up sensationally – it really stood up well to the hit I took into the wall. Coincidentally, I was wearing some sensors that were logging my heart rate and a few other things. The guys told me some of the numbers they saw on the instruments were pretty amazing in terms of what my body went through.

The end result: yours truly sitting in less than splendid isolation amid the wreckage of a car that was supposed to be mine at the end of the season.

Seb's very quick at Valencia and he enjoyed a much happier day than I did.

It was a good day for the McLaren boys as well, but they were obviously keen to see what makes the RB6 so fast.

So off I went to the medical centre. I've had a bit of experience there, and I couldn't help thinking, 'Here we go again!' I'd bashed my toe on the top of the chassis when I landed – there's no padding in the lower half of the cockpit to prevent the toes hitting the top of the monocoque when a freak accident like this occurs – and my foot was really sore. I had some swelling in my joints, and over the next few weeks had a few headaches, but otherwise I pulled up pretty well. Ferrari Team Principal Stefano Domenicali put his arm around me as we were leaving the track and said, 'Mark, health is everything.' He was right then and he still is.

I caught up with Heikki in the medical centre and said, 'Mate, what were you doing? You were five seconds off the pace and one

The only thing that was going to lift me after my coming together with the Lotus was one of these.

Heikki's mirrors were clearly about as much use as his shades!

The incident left Christian Horner with some awkward questions to answer from the likes of journos Mark Hughes and Johnny Noble.

Seb was the one to take a sackful of points away from Spain this time.

Mind you, Bruno Senna may not have been picking up too much on the track but he seems to be doing all right off it ...

of the quickest cars in the pack was behind you. I've been in a Minardi: it's quicker for you to roll out of the throttle, let me through and off we go. For you to start fighting and blocking and thinking you're going to hold out a car at that level, well ... That's how the crash happened.'

I'm sure he saw it differently.

I was annoyed that our points tally took such a big hit, but what really upset me was what happened to the car – chassis 4 – the one in which I'd won at Barcelona and Monaco. As part of the re-negotiations for 2011, the team was going to give it to me at the end of the season. The boys were really attached to it as well, and wrote a message on the wreckage before it was sent away to

Not today it didn't, Seb, and it wouldn't at Silverstone, either!

be crunched: 'You gave me the best day of my life, thank you, and today you also saved my mate.' I'll probably take the British Grand Prix–winning car now because it's got the F-duct on it and I want everything! But it was a pity about chassis 4: I had destroyed Seb in that car, and he'd won a race with it, too, so it was very, very special.

Wish I could say the same about Valencia ...

GREAT
BRITAIN
TWO INTO ONE WON'T GO

GREAT BRITAIN

Pole Position:
Sebastian Vettel (RBR–Renault),
1:29.615 = 236.652 km/h
[MW front row, 1:29.758]

Fastest Lap:
Fernando Alonso (Ferrari),
1:30.874 = 233.373 km/h, lap 52
[MW: 1:32.364, lap 45]

Podium:
1. Mark Webber (RBR–Renault)
2. Lewis Hamilton (McLaren–Mercedes)
3. Nico Rosberg (Mercedes GP)

Drivers' World Championship:
1. Hamilton 145 points
2. Button 133
3. Webber 128

Constructors' World Championship:
1. McLaren–Mercedes 278 points
2. RBR–Renault 249
3. Ferrari 165

Races are won and lost in the first
few seconds these days. There
was no way I was letting anyone
else get away from me this time.

Race Date:	11 July 2010
Circuit Name:	Silverstone
Number of Laps:	52
Circuit Length:	5.901 km
Race Distance:	306.852 km
Lap Record:	1:30.874 – F Alonso (2010)

TWO INTO ONE WON'T GO

'Not bad for a number two driver.' This was the phrase that triggered headlines after I won the 2010 British Grand Prix in what might be called 'controversial circumstances'. I should have thrown in some foul language; if I'd said something colourful, it would never have gone to air. But I was a good boy that day and my comment ended up making the international television feed. That's what sport is like: it gets emotional, and we should be glad it does. Thankfully,

the emotion that Sunday in July was very different from what I had just been through in Spain.

I was feeling fit and focused in spite of the distractions in the lead-up to Silverstone: a Red Bull UK appearance at the Milton Keynes kart track, British and Brazilian media visits to the factory, dinner with former Australian cricket captain Steve Waugh at Lord's (a magnificent experience for any Aussie), and an unusual practice pit stop performed outside Big Ben in the

Not the red lights a racing
driver expects to see!

I may not be an Englishman, but these guys seem to have taken the Aussie who lives nearby to their hearts.

The Festival of Speed at Goodwood House was stressful with so many people asking about the Valencia crash, but it was great to meet Lord March (left) and have some competitive fun with Adrian.

centre of London. There was also the annual Festival of Speed at Goodwood House in Sussex. This is a wonderful celebration of all things motorsport, and it gave me the chance to sample some machinery I'd only ever seen on TV. It was fun, but punishing, too, because people were constantly referring to the crash in Valencia, constantly reminding me of it when all I wanted to do was move on.

Extracurricular activities are part and parcel of a modern sportsperson's life, but with the commitments fulfilled, it was nice to finally get back into the RB6. You never quite know how it's going to feel after a big shunt like the one I had in Spain. Happily, I felt fine right away. Silverstone had a new circuit layout, so we had to get our heads around that, but I was pleased to see they'd kept most of our favourite sections. I didn't get out for my last practice run on Friday so I had to do my high fuel work on Saturday, which meant I was running a heavy car.

And then the trouble really started ...

Seb and I had been given new front wings on Friday and the boys from the aerodynamic department were keen for us to use them. We were happy to do so, but it was tricky trying to work out what settings you needed to use and how to set up the aerodynamic configuration of the rest of the car. There were some other complications as well, so we took Friday night to digest it all.

In the end it was a no-brainer and come Saturday morning we both wanted to run the new wings. So we said, 'Let's just get on with it; they're better. End of story.'

Well, not quite ...

Qualifying at Silverstone – the body language tells you I'm not too happy ...

Seb's new wing failed in the first session, and mine had a small bonding issue on one of the sections and looked as if it might not be useable either. So we decided to revert back to the older design. But then it turned out my new wing was fine ... and the team elected to give it to Seb. I wasn't happy. It was the first time the team had ever been in the position where they had two drivers but only one part: a unique situation, and one that was handled 'interestingly' from my perspective.

This was the crucial thing – getting ahead of Seb in the opening metres of the race.

After the top ten qualifying shoot-out, we both ended up on the front row of the grid. Seb got pole and I got P2, missing out on the top spot by 0.14 of a second. It looked like whoever started on pole would have the best chance of winning the race. Going into qualifying I hadn't felt that I had the same car or the same opportunity, and that was disappointing. I had a short meeting with Christian and Adrian before I went home on Saturday night, and I'd cooled down a little by then. I think the outburst that came on Sunday would have come on Saturday if I'd got pole. But timing is everything and I needed to get a certain job done before I could express myself more forcefully.

When I woke up on Sunday morning things were worse. I felt used. Maybe I did

go a bit over the top, maybe I was being sensitive, but a stance had to be taken and that could only come from me. Just like Race 7 in Turkey, this was another occasion where I needed to make my presence felt. What if Seb had passed me in Istanbul and disappeared? Who knows where the momentum would have been within the team, and how things might have snowballed from there. In the end he hadn't, and at Silverstone I again needed to remind everyone: hey, I'm here!

So that's what I did. I had a good start, won the first corner, and from there the race was pretty uneventful!

Of course you want to win every Grand Prix, but the 2010 Silverstone race was sweet for all sorts of reasons, not least

Here's a manoeuvre I'm starting to perfect!

because I've been based in England a long time, I've been with the British Racing Drivers' Club (BRDC) a long time and Silverstone feels more like my 'home' race than Albert Park. I'd also won there in all sorts of cars, so to finally manage it in a Formula 1 car was a wonderful feeling.

Despite my win, several key people in the team weren't too keen to come near me that Sunday afternoon! If you're the one winning races, who can argue with that? Red Bull was experiencing unprecedented growing pains and was learning how to handle not one but two drivers desperate – and capable – of getting pole. It was a new situation for Christian and he found himself in an awkward position having to make hard decisions before the race. We all learn from our mistakes and only experience can make us wiser.

Ultimately, I think it was a positive learning curve for the team because now we've been through this type of scenario we can say, 'This is how the rule should be applied.' Maybe I lost out on Saturday because everyone thought Seb couldn't handle it if he didn't get the new front wing. Imagine what it might have been like if it had been him in my place – they might have had a full-scale meltdown on their hands. So perhaps it was easier to say, 'Let's do it to Mark. He's stronger, he'll be fine, he'll get on with it, he always does.'

Well, yes, I will, but don't test it too far, guys ...

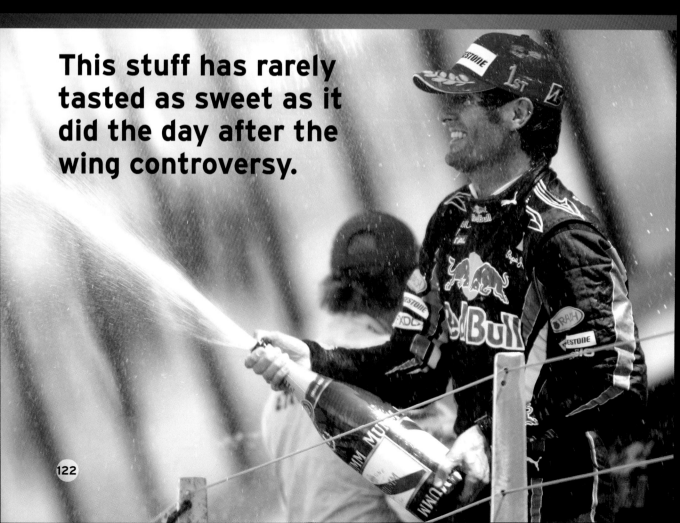

This stuff has rarely tasted as sweet as it did the day after the wing controversy.

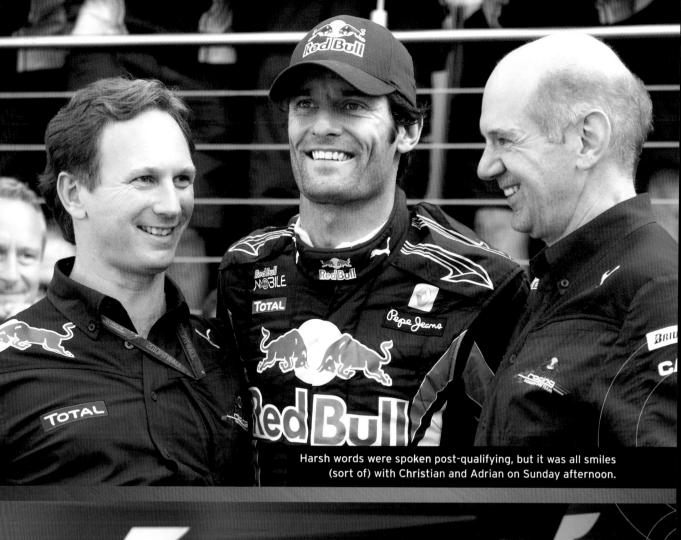

Harsh words were spoken post-qualifying, but it was all smiles (sort of) with Christian and Adrian on Sunday afternoon.

Jenson is one of the local heroes.

NTANDER BRITISH GRAND PRIX

123

Are those storm clouds gathering as Ferrari heads for a Hockenheim one–two?

GERMANY
NOT IN THE FIGHT

GERMANY

Pole Position:
Sebastian Vettel (RBR–Renault),
1:13.791 = 223.149 km/h
[MW P4, 1:14.347]

Fastest Lap:
Sebastian Vettel (RBR–Renault),
1:15.824 = 217.166 km/h, lap 67
[MW: 1:16.678, lap 57]

Podium:
1. Fernando Alonso (Ferrari)
2. Felipe Massa (Ferrari)
3. Sebastian Vettel (RBR–Renault)
[MW P6]

Drivers' World Championship:
1. Hamilton 157 points
2. Button 143
3. Webber 136

Constructors' World Championship:
1. McLaren–Mercedes 300 points
2. RBR–Renault 272
3. Ferrari 208

Race Date: 25 July 2010
Circuit Name: Hockenheimring
Number of Laps: 67
Circuit Length: 4.574 km
Race Distance: 306.458 km
Lap Record: 1:13.780 – K Räikkönen (2004)

NOT IN THE FIGHT

Just over a year after my very first Grand Prix win at the Nürburgring in the Eifel Mountains we were back in Germany, this time at the Hockenheim circuit in the Rhine Valley. But with the change of venue came a change of fortunes: I was never really in the fight and, in any case, the race was overshadowed by another classic Formula 1 fiasco.

Let's deal with my weekend first. For the first time since Bahrain back in mid-March, I didn't make the front row of the grid. In Q3 I ran wide into Turn 1, lost my last lap, and as a result was bumped to fourth. Seb took pole while Fernando and Felipe in the two Ferraris started second and third respectively.

When the five red lights went out, Seb hesitated on the line and then had to do his best to squeeze out Fernando. Felipe took the opportunity and went round them both to grab the lead. Although I got away reasonably well, Lewis's McLaren used its straight-line advantage to get by me on the way down to the Turn 6 hairpin. We had a good fight early on – he looked uncomfortable on the softer option tyres – but his sheer speed on the straights meant I just couldn't clear him. He stayed out a lap longer than I did during the pit stops, laps 13 to 14, and when I rejoined the race and got stuck in traffic, he was able to get the jump on me.

By the time all the front-runners had pitted, I was down in sixth, behind both

McLarens. The car was using too much oil and I had to modify my downshift patterns and stop using the F-duct, so there was really no chance of challenging Jenson for fifth. But grabbing some points was better than retiring with none. In the end I just managed to get the car home and had to switch it off as I crossed the line.

But the 2010 German Grand Prix wasn't about Red Bull ...

Looking back, I think Fernando had been frustrated with the situation within Ferrari as early as the Australian Grand Prix. Sure, there were times when he was forced to sit behind Felipe because of unavoidable circumstances, but there were also times when the team could have got a better

The weekend started well enough with Casio launching their limited edition Red Bull Racing watch.

result had Fernando been released to set his own pace. Let's not beat about the bush: teammates releasing each other due to different race strategies has been going on every year for the last decade. It's done in the interests of the team. For example, if I'm on a three-stop strategy and my teammate is on a two-stop strategy, then the team should release me because I'm going to be quicker

FORMULA 1° GROSSER PREIS SANTANDER VON DEUTSCHLAND 2010

I was the odd man out among the home drivers – but at least they spoke to me!

at that point of the race. Of course, it might all equal out by the end and the best guy will win. The ideal situation is for the team to have both cars doing the fastest lap times they can – all the time.

But because we no longer stop to refuel (only to change tyres), there's inevitably less strategy involved these days, and the incident at Hockenheim was the first of its kind I'd seen this season. Some people might argue that if both a team's cars are running close together, a decision must be made about which driver gets to pit first, because whoever that is will have the advantage of fresh tyres and a good chance of jumping the other driver. This is generally discussed in the pre-race briefing. But going into Hockenheim, Ferrari had other

issues to deal with. Fernando and Felipe had collided at Silverstone and this no doubt would have added to what is normally a highly pressured situation.

So there they are with around 18 laps to go, running one–two. Felipe is in front but Fernando is quicker. Felipe gets the call from his race engineer Rob Smedley. 'Can you confirm that Fernando is faster?' Rob asks. I translate this as: 'Show us what you can do in the next few laps: if you can pull out a gap, then the victory's yours. If you can't, then we need to release Fernando.' I wouldn't call it race-fixing, but rather 'team orders' (which have been banned since 2002). Felipe has done nothing wrong, and neither has Fernando. But it looks terrible when you see it and, more importantly on this occasion, hear it on the live international TV feed.

Felipe drove a fantastic first stint and if he had put in a similarly good second stint he probably would have won the race. But he didn't, and once he began to struggle, Fernando began having a nibble here and there. Fernando had been in this situation before and he must have been thinking, 'Bloody hell, let me go – I can get a third or a fourth out of this instead of being held up behind Felipe.' They would have discussed the possibility of this happening before the race, and Felipe would have gone in with his eyes wide open. He knew what he needed to do; it wouldn't have come as a surprise to him.

I was pretty focused, but at Hockenheim sixth was as high as I would manage.

Off the front row for the first time since Bahrain.

Maybe I was just getting too much advice!

This is the way Ferrari and others race, and it's been like this for 50 years. If they'd been running three cars, the same thing would have happened; if you had just one there'd be no team orders because you'd be simply telling your driver to do his best.

Ferrari made the call a bit early on, but it was probably the correct one. They certainly could have disguised it better, though. Felipe could have come in, had a slow pit stop and the team could've said, 'Sorry, mate, we made a meal of your stop.' Fernando could've then overtaken him in the pits and gone on to win. No one outside the team would've known it was the plan all along. To their credit, they gave Felipe a fair crack at winning, but when he couldn't pull it off, it was up to

Rob Smedley to make that infamous phone call. He couldn't resist saying 'Sorry' before he hung up and this of course got Ferrari in trouble with the stewards. They copped a €100,000 fine and were hauled before the World Motor Sport Council's disciplinary panel. They escaped further penalty, though, and the team orders rule is now under review.

Ultimately, the fastest driver won the 2010 German Grand Prix and, from where I stood, it wasn't a disaster that it was Ferrari that collected the points. We thought McLaren would be strong in Germany, but they weren't. It seemed a different rival was emerging ... and I was glad we only had a week to wait before we got the chance to fight back.

Felipe led the race fair and square in a brilliant opening stint.

Fernando was fastest on the day
and it was logical he should win.

It was Rob Smedley, Felipe's race engineer, who had to make the call with the bad news.

It's not hard to figure out how Felipe felt about it.

HUNGARY

Pole Position:
Sebastian Vettel (RBR–Renault),
1:18.773 = 200.215 km/h
[MW front row, 1:19.184]

Fastest Lap:
Sebastian Vettel (RBR–Renault),
1:22.362 = 191.491 km/h, lap 70
[MW: 1:22.651, lap 46]

Podium:
1. Mark Webber (RBR–Renault)
2. Fernando Alonso (Ferrari)
3. Sebastian Vettel (RBR–Renault)

Drivers' World Championship:
1. Webber 161 points
2. Hamilton 157
3. Vettel 151

Constructors' World Championship:
1. RBR–Renault 312 points
2. McLaren–Mercedes 304
3. Ferrari 238

HUNGARY
A BIT OF A GIFT

RACE 12 >>> BUDAPEST

Race Date:	1 August 2010
Circuit Name:	Hungaroring
Number of Laps:	70
Circuit Length:	4.381 km
Race Distance:	306.630 km
Lap Record:	1:19.071 – M Schumacher (2004)

A BIT OF A GIFT

The 2010 Hungarian Grand Prix marked a double milestone: it was the 100th Grand Prix for Red Bull Racing and, amazingly, the 150th start for me in F1. Looking back, we couldn't have asked for anything better than the way this special weekend worked out.

It was fitting that it was in the home of the twin cities of Buda and Pest that we would have twin success for the Red Bull–Renaults with another qualifying front-row lockout on Saturday. The RB6 really surprised us – we couldn't believe how phenomenal it was round the track. In the end, Seb snatched pole, but my side of the garage was right up there. More importantly, the rest of the field, led by

Fernando's Ferrari, were eight-tenths of a second behind us! This was definitely our strongest circuit so far this season.

But what soon became clear – and a little bit frustrating – is that P2 at the Hungaroring is not the ideal position to start the race. The left side of the track is very dirty and the run down to the first corner is the second longest of the season after Barcelona. Nevertheless, Seb deserved to get pole, and my second lap in Q3 wasn't as clean as it might have been.

After qualifying, I remarked how important it was to get your tyres right in order to nail your lap. I hadn't prepared them properly for my crack at pole, coming up behind first Lewis then Robert, but on

It was crucial that my pit stop took full advantage of all the hard work done.

Another pivotal moment for me: Seb comes in to take a drive-through penalty for his safety car mistake.

137

Sunday my tyre strategy would make a huge difference to the outcome of the Grand Prix. It turned out to be a prophetic comment.

For our first stint the plan was to beat Ferrari by isolating Felipe. Fernando got away well at the start, but we were happy to see him pull away from Felipe – it meant I could take on the Spaniard one-on-one in the pits and not have Felipe trying to undercut me at the same time. To no one's surprise, Seb was fast disappearing up the road, so I just concentrated on looking after the car and the tyres, and waited

This was the consequence: one happy Red Bull, one not so happy!

for a round of pit stops to try to take on Fernando.

But then, as is so often the way in Formula 1, the whole race got turned on its head.

About 13 laps in, a sizeable chunk of Force India driver Vitantonio Liuzzi's endplate fell off. Michael had clipped it at the start of the race, but it had taken its time to come adrift. The safety car was called out, and immediately Seb and Fernando dived into the pits. I'd been praying for this to happen. Ciaron was straight on the phone, saying, 'Stay out! Stay out!' As soon as I saw Fernando's car head into the pits, I thought, 'Right, now we can do something different.'

In fact, I now had to put in 40 laps from hell and I did wonder whether the option tyres would stand up to the pressure. In

FORMULA 1™ ENI MAGYAR NAGYDÍJ 2010

order to be able to pit safely, change tyres and still maintain the lead, we needed to open up a gap of 18 seconds or more on whoever was in second place ... If we could manage that, we stood a good chance of winning the race.

As the safety car's lights went out, indicating we were about to restart, Seb began dropping back. I was ahead of him, running in first place, and had my car primed and ready to go. I thought he must have had a problem with his gearbox or his brakes. Or maybe he was trying to screw Fernando by backing him up and giving me a nice jump-start? Hang on; he'd never do that! Whatever the reason, Seb fell back too far, made a mess of the restart, and was bound to get in trouble with the stewards. The rule is that when a safety car is on track,

you must stay within 10 car lengths of the car in front of you.

I was focused on what I had to do and told Ciaron that I wasn't interested in Vettel; they needed to give me the gap to Fernando, lap by lap. There was no way I was going to get 25 seconds on Seb before the end of the race – he was just too quick. Then I saw on the big screen that I was at the top of the track just as Seb was coming onto the front straight and I thought, 'He's going to cop a drive-through penalty for that.' He did and served it after lap 32, putting him in third place and Fernando

Our cause was helped when Lewis had a gearbox issue that left him a spectator.

Like me, Fernando knew how important those tyres were at the Hungaroring.

into second. The race was now mine to win, but it did mean that for the remainder I'd have to drive flat out ... without going off the edge.

Although my front left tyre wasn't enjoying itself, particularly through the last corner, we had the luxury of staying out longer to extend the margin so the boys didn't have to panic when I finally came into the pits. To do all that work over the past 40-odd minutes and for one of them to fumble a wheel nut would have been a nightmare ... for us all. But by lap 38 we had the gap we needed, so we added to it, and by lap 43 we'd pulled out a comfortable 24-second lead. I pitted, rejoined the race still out in front, and controlled things from there.

It was a brilliant team effort – our strategy, the car, me and the boys in the pit lane were all spot-on – and the decisions we made across the board earned us our

victory. Some people reckon I was lucky and yes, it *was* a bit of a gift, but I've not had many of them in F1 and I was happy to take it. It was a new scenario for me. I did something different from the rest of the field and that's exactly what was needed to win. I had to put in some decent, consistent laps and pick off the back-markers – I think I lapped about 800 Lotuses in that race (thankfully Heikki Kovalainen's a lot better now and gets out the way!). Coincidentally, our main rivals had a rough time of it: Lewis retired with a suspected gearbox failure and Jenson finished down in eighth. But I'm happy to take that, too: this special weekend in Hungary put Red Bull Racing ahead of McLaren in the Constructors' Championship – and an Aussie bloke by the name of Webber up front in the Drivers'.

Every picture tells a story ...

Celebrating the 25th running
of the race in Hungary.

Milestones all round: 300 races for the
Sauber team led by team owner Peter Sauber
(third from left, holding the pitboard).

The things we do ...   And the things you see! Russell Crowe he's not ...

It was great to share the moment with another of Red Bull's hardest-working people, Darren Nicholls.

D. NICHOLLS

M. WEBBER

Spa-Francorchamps: the thrill
of the famous Eau Rouge corner,
the spills in the weather!

BELGIUM

WEATHERING THE STORM

BELGIUM

Pole Position:
Mark Webber (RBR–Renault),
1:45.778 = 238.370 km/h

Fastest Lap:
Lewis Hamilton (McLaren–Mercedes),
1:49.069 = 231.178 km/h, lap 32
[MW: 1:49.935, lap 32]

Podium:
1. Lewis Hamilton (McLaren–Mercedes)
2. Mark Webber (RBR–Renault)
3. Robert Kubica (Renault)

Drivers' World Championship:
1. Hamilton 182 points
2. Webber 179
3. Vettel 151

Constructors' World Championship:
1. RBR–Renault 330 points
2. McLaren–Mercedes 329
3. Ferrari 250

Race Date:	29 August 2010
Circuit Name:	Circuit de Spa-Francorchamps
Number of Laps:	44
Circuit Length:	7.004 km
Race Distance:	308.052 km
Lap Record:	1:45.108 – K Räikkönen (2004)

WEATHERING THE STORM

I f the Hungaroring was one of our strongest tracks of 2010, we knew the next two were going to be some of our weakest. The great traditional European venues of Spa-Francorchamps in Belgium and Monza in Italy are both wonderful tracks and places I love. But we were worried their long, sweeping straights would make the RB6 vulnerable to the hunters behind us.

The mid-season break after Hungary was good. It was a bonus finishing the first half of the F1 year with a solid result and you can't get more solid than being the Championship leader! On the Sunday before the Belgian Grand Prix, I took my brother-in-law to watch Fulham play Manchester United at Craven Cottage and was thrilled to meet one of the greatest names in English soccer history, Sir Bobby Charlton. Not only that, I also got to have dinner with Fulham's Aussie goalkeeper, Mark Schwarzer.

When we arrived at Spa the weather forecast looked dismal for the whole weekend. Friday practice wasn't a complete wash-out, but we didn't get very much done. On Saturday, we knew we'd have to take some risks to position ourselves well; if it's a wet start visibility is critical. You can't afford to think, 'It's going to be a long race, I can start fifth or sixth and see what happens.' You need to be up the front no matter what you open the curtains to on Sunday morning.

Qualifying turned out to be just as challenging as we'd imagined. In changing

Rubens Barrichello (standing third from the left) is one of F1's most recognisable faces. It should be – this was his 300th Grand Prix!

We kept my 34th birthday in the family.

Uh-oh ... a start-line glitch and
I'm buried, back in seventh.

conditions, it's easy to get knocked out early, so I had to put in some key laps in order to make it through. I was 11th at one stage in Q2, but I had another lap up my sleeve and thought, 'It's not going to be easy, I'm on the bubble.' I knew how important it was to finish that lap cleanly.

Going into Q3, Ciaron gave me a sensational piece of advice. 'This lap – the first one – could be it: don't build up to the next one because you might not get it.' At 7.004 kilometres Spa is one of the longest circuits on the calendar and you need to get everything right, starting with Turn 1, the right-hand hairpin called La Source. Pinch a front tyre there and you've bombed the whole lap. When you get it right, though, it's extra special.

My first lap was good and Ciaron got straight on the radio. 'You're there, you're on pole.' I went round again, but it had rained in

the meantime and, being at the top of a hill, La Source was the wettest part of the track and I lost three-tenths of a second there. The next lap after that wasn't any better. Would my first one be enough? It turned out that it was. Lewis drove brilliantly to get on the front row and only missed pole by 0.085 of a second – a phenomenal effort on a drenched track. Seb didn't improve on my time so that settled the grid: me on pole, Lewis on P2, Robert Kubica on P3 and Seb back on P4.

We'd had a small problem with the hydraulics on my car during qualifying and the boys were nervous about how it would pan out on Sunday. They suggested I do two laps before lining up on the grid – not ideal for our preparation – and so I told Ciaron, 'Let's just do one – if everything's okay I can pull onto the back of the grid – we don't have to do the other lap and the start guys will be

A nice birthday gift for me when Seb lost control and collided with Jenson ...

One of the title-chasing quintet making an early exit.

happy. But as he correctly pointed out, we'd still need to put fuel in the car for another lap in case it *wasn't* all right, and we didn't want to have to carry that extra fuel round for the race.

So I did the two laps and the car seemed fine, but my start of the formation lap was rubbish. I made an adjustment on the way round to the real start, but when the red lights went out, bang! It happened again. I was on the back foot straight away and by the time we came out of the first corner, I was stuck in seventh. At tight circuits like Monaco or Barcelona, on a typically scorching-hot day, this is where you'd finish the Grand Prix. But sometimes uncertain weather can come to the rescue, and on that Sunday at Spa, I knew I was still in the hunt ...

So I hung in there. Jenson held a few people up in the opening stages, and then

Seb crashed into him? Seb obviously had too much brake pressure when the car was under lateral load, and with the momentum he couldn't save it. That earned him another drive-through penalty.

With Seb and Jenson gone and Lewis out in front, there was just Robert Kubica – who was then running second – to contend with. I kept him honest – honest enough to make a mistake in his pit stop. He was distracted by having to adjust settings on the steering wheel as he came in and slightly overshot it.

When I pitted, the boys did another great job, getting me turned around and back out on the intermediate tyres in just 3.6 seconds. Things continued to fall our way when Fernando lost his Ferrari at Turn 7, the right-hander known as Malmédy, which brought the safety car out briefly. As I was waiting for the restart behind Lewis, I thought, 'Okay, if

To go or not to go? I considered having a shot at Lewis when the safety car came in but then thought better of it.

No denying it, Lewis put in a sensational performance in the challenging Spa conditions.

It's a hell of a track, but you have to stay focused.

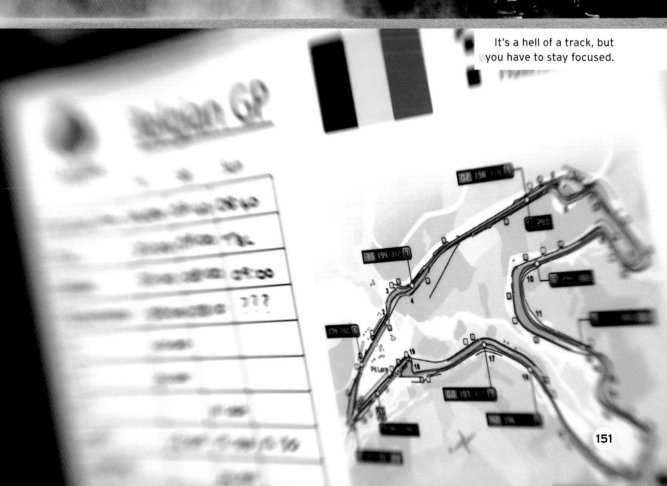

Robert Kubica's little pit lane hiccup also helped me out.

I can get a good run through Turn 2 – Eau Rouge – I might have a crack at him.' But it'd be risky. In hindsight, I could have gone through Eau Rouge even faster. I went through as fast as I dared, on what I thought was the limit at the time. I put the pressure on but didn't quite get there and the rest of the race was a stalemate between Lewis and me.

Second place at Spa-Francorchamps was a great result, irrespective of how it actually panned out. Who knew what would happen by season's end? The 18 points I earned might make all the difference. Although Lewis enjoyed the top spot on the podium and regained the lead in the Drivers' Championship, I was happy to come away from one of our most challenging venues just three points in arrears. The hunt was well and truly on.

No, I'm not refusing to listen – in fact, former racing driver Dr Helmut Marko was very nice to me after the race!

It wasn't a victory, but there was no telling how important this Spa result might prove to be.

ITALY

Pole Position:
Fernando Alonso (Ferrari),
1:21.962 = 254.861 km/h
[MW P4, 1:22.433]

Fastest Lap:
Fernando Alonso (Ferrari),
1:24.139 = 247.178 km/h, lap 52
[MW: 1:24.278, lap 52]

Podium:
1. Fernando Alonso (Ferrari)
2. Jenson Button (McLaren–Mercedes)
3. Felipe Massa (Ferrari)
[MW P6]

Drivers' World Championship:
1. Webber 187 points
2. Hamilton 182
3. Alonso 166

Constructors' World Championship:
1. RBR–Renault 350 points
2. McLaren–Mercedes 347
3. Ferrari 290

Monza mayhem – a Ferrari had just won the Italian Grand Prix and the *Tifosi* were going mad!

ITALY
THE INCREDIBLE HULK

RACE 14 >>> MONZA

Race Date:	12 September 2010
Circuit Name:	Autodromo di Monza
Number of Laps:	53
Circuit Length:	5.793 km
Race Distance:	306.720 km
Lap Record:	1:21.046 – R Barrichello (2004)

THE INCREDIBLE HULK

The Italian Grand Prix is one of the oldest events on the motor racing calendar and the track at the Villa Reale Park north of Milan is everything the F1 traditionalist loves. Work began on the original circuit back in 1922 and it has been rebuilt many times over the years. Formula 1 cars no longer race along the high-speed oval bankings they used in the 50s and 60s, but the charm of the long straights, the Lesmo curves and the setting in the royal park still make it a magical place to drive.

That said, it was always going to be our toughest venue of the year. Monza demands exactly what the RB6 is *not* good at –

Sometimes things don't go right, as I found out in practice, so a helping hand from these guys was welcome.

Good job we had time for a friendly chat before the race: winning at Monza made Fernando my new public enemy number one.

Even movie stars like having their picture taken on a Grand Prix grid!

157

accelerating away from mega low-speed corners, up to seventh, and back down again – and we knew we'd be particularly vulnerable on the big run down to Turn 9, the Ascari chicane. But I thought, 'Nothing's impossible'; we'd do our best and see what we could come away with.

It had taken a long time to build the house and accrue the points, and for a while it looked as if the wreckers might have moved in. I didn't feel settled at Friday practice and on Saturday morning I lost some crucial running time because of a water leak and an airbox fire. This was all the more frustrating because overnight Ciaron and I had changed a few things on the car. Initially they worked well and we were more competitive, but we had to keep adjusting things and by the time

qualifying came around I hadn't even tested Bridgestone's option tyres!

Monza is the spiritual home of Ferrari and the stands are always packed with their loyal supporters, aka the *Tifosi*. Much to their delight, Fernando grabbed the team's first pole since the Brazilian Grand Prix in 2008, while Jenson got P2 and Felipe in the other Ferrari got P3. I managed to cobble together a pretty decent lap in Q3 and made it onto the second row in P4. Lewis was in P5, while Seb got P6.

On race day, my start wasn't too bad – it was certainly a lot better than at Spa – but I

It must have been strange for Michael to come back to Monza and not be in a Ferrari ...

Doesn't Nico Hulkenberg look all sweetness and light?

But you try getting past him when he takes 101 different lines through a Monza chicane!

159

It was a day for the men in red, with a Ferrari one-three finish.

had some wheel-spin on the dirty side of the track and Nico Rosberg squeezed past me on the run to the first chicane. Then I was in the wrong lane for the chicane itself and got creamed when I exited, with Robert Kubica, Nico Hulkenberg and Seb all blowing by on the outside. I was still on the defensive when the other Mercedes came past as we cleared the second chicane, and so after one lap I was down in ninth! I thought, 'It's a long way

I had to settle in, put my head down and do the hard yards. Michael Schumacher – a five-time winner at Monza – was my first target. We had a good scrap before I dealt with him on lap 6, which meant the 'new Schumacher' – Seb – was up next. I could see he was having brake problems out of the Ascari chicane and I was past him by lap 20. But then came the Incredible Hulk. As far as I'm aware, a Williams is no bigger than a Red Bull or any of the other cars on the grid, but it sure as hell seemed that way this year.

Nico Hulkenberg debuted in F1 in 2010 as the GP2 champion, so clearly he's no slouch. But he had a 'particular' way of dealing with the Monza chicanes. At one point it looked as if he was straight-lining them every second lap. In fact, from where I sat, it looked like he had *two* driving lines: one on track, the other off it! I was getting pretty angry, stuck in seventh behind him, and kept expecting him to be pinged by the stewards for cutting the chicanes and gaining an advantage. Apparently Race Director Charlie Whiting did issue a warning, but no further action was taken.

I was losing time, so my next option was to try to jump him during the pit stops. That didn't work either and we exited with Robert Kubica's Renault between us. So at this traditional venue we had to resort to a traditional method: overtaking on the track. I got Robert first, but in the end I had to be aggressive to get past Nico round the outside on the run down to the second chicane.

But my troubles weren't over yet. Seb had been due for a tyre stop around the quarter-distance mark, but he was still running in

back from here; we'll be lucky to get away with poor starts two races in a row.'

Mind you, if my start was poor, Lewis's was a disaster. He was leading the Drivers' Championship when we arrived in Italy, but he blew it within seconds. Unsurprisingly, he got away well, but he tried a move on Felipe at the first chicane that was never going to stick. Just like that, one key rival was out of the race.

The big boss, Red Bull magnate Dietrich Mateschitz, came to watch us race at Monza.

clear air in fourth place. When he finally came in with just one lap to go, the other Nico – Rosberg in the Mercedes – got stuck in traffic and backed both of us up. There was no time to attack, so sixth was my lot for the weekend. Seb held on to fourth, while Fernando, Jenson and Felipe finished the race in the same positions they started it and got to spray the champagne on the podium.

It was a strange Grand Prix. Our strategy was upside down, and trying to clear Hulkenberg was difficult. To be fair, he raced as hard as he could for his team and I caught him in the end, but it was frustrating. I felt we could have got more out of the weekend than we did. And not only that, a bloke by the name of Alonso in a bright red car was really beginning to make his presence felt ...

Flavio Briatore also put in an appearance – and of course there were deals to be done.

It was a
weekend
that saw
a swing in
the drivers'
standings
- and this
time Lewis
lost out.

There's always something to reflect on at Monza ...

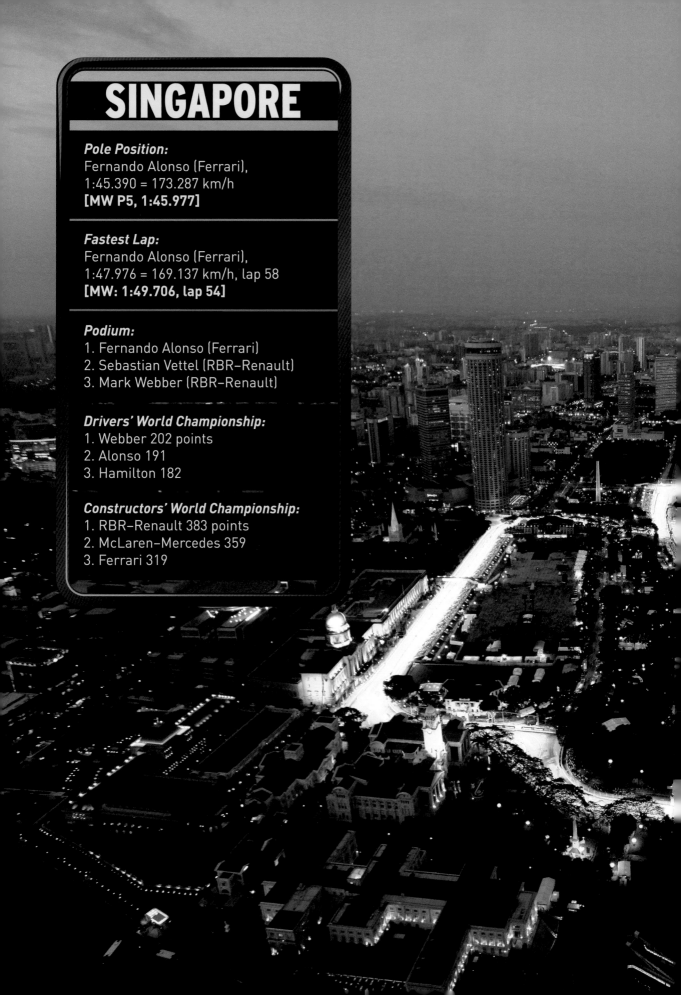

SINGAPORE

Pole Position:
Fernando Alonso (Ferrari),
1:45.390 = 173.287 km/h
[MW P5, 1:45.977]

Fastest Lap:
Fernando Alonso (Ferrari),
1:47.976 = 169.137 km/h, lap 58
[MW: 1:49.706, lap 54]

Podium:
1. Fernando Alonso (Ferrari)
2. Sebastian Vettel (RBR–Renault)
3. Mark Webber (RBR–Renault)

Drivers' World Championship:
1. Webber 202 points
2. Alonso 191
3. Hamilton 182

Constructors' World Championship:
1. RBR–Renault 383 points
2. McLaren–Mercedes 359
3. Ferrari 319

SINGAPORE

A BIG CALL AND A CLOSE CALL

Singapore has added a brilliant
new dimension to Formula 1.

Race Date:	26 September 2010
Circuit Name:	Marina Bay Street Circuit
Number of Laps:	61
Circuit Length:	5.073 km
Race Distance:	309.316 km
Lap Record:	1:47.976 – F Alonso (2010)

A BIG CALL AND A CLOSE CALL

After the challenging venues of Spa and Monza, Singapore's Marina Bay Street Circuit should have edged our RB6 back into competitive territory. But as I wrote earlier in this book, there are still a few tracks around the world that I haven't quite mastered. Singapore is one of them.

The weekend started well enough when I went fastest in the first practice session and then second fastest behind Seb in the next session. But I'd be less than honest if I said I was totally comfortable. Going into qualifying I had to work on the tricky last sector, turns 18 to 19, and all that stuff through there, but it turned out to be my best. I ended up with

fifth on the grid and probably could have got fourth, but I need to adapt to the changing conditions in Singapore better and adjust my driving style to suit it. That's something for next time.

We'd been monitoring the weather all weekend, watching huge black clouds roll in and out and dodging intermittent showers, but Sunday brought us beautiful clear blue skies. For the race start under lights at 8 pm the weather was still good, and pretty much everybody except Lewis got off the grid cleanly. I was behind Jenson, who started from P4, which wasn't ideal. Out of the five drivers vying for the Championship, he's

We were watching the skies
all Friday and Saturday.

For Ferrari it was a tale of two
drivers – and Felipe was the
one who missed out.

167

It's never been 'my' Singapore, but despite the lowly grid position, I got something from the Lion City this year.

Never in the race, but one of the key cars on the night ...

Mercedes-Benz

Allianz

///AMG

Lewis tries to pass me on the outside of Turn 7, I hold my line, and we touch.

Danny Sullivan – pictured on the right talking to Adrian Newey – is a former Indianapolis 500 winner and Tyrrell F1 driver. Thankfully he knows a racing incident when he sees one.

Once Robert Kubica bolted on new tyres, he was the hottest man on track in the closing stages of the race.

The only man hotter than Robert Kubica was Heikki Kovalainen, who kept his cool admirably when his Lotus erupted in flames right at the end.

the least comfy with a heavy fuel load and is prone to slowing things down. But it didn't matter: on lap 2, Vitantonio Liuzzi's Force India collided with Nick Heidfeld's BMW Sauber. And out came the safety car.

While the marshals removed Liuzzi's broken Force India, we tried to figure out the best course of action. Before the race, we'd worked out what we would do if there was a safety car period on lap 7 or 12; but an incident this early on meant a change of plan. We were a bit marginal on brakes and weren't going to be all that effective attacking with a heavy car, so Christian told the team to bring me into the pits and gamble on switching to the hard prime tyres. I was unsure – it was a big call to run such a long stint on those tyres – but it turned out to be an inspired decision.

I rejoined the race in tenth place behind Kamui Kobayashi in the other BMW Sauber. I had to be careful as he was driving on the limit – just missing walls and jumping kerbs – but on lap 7 I caught him. Next I took on Michael and managed to pass him on lap 11; but then came Rubens Barrichello, whose Williams was working well, particularly out of turns 3 and 5.

By this stage, Fernando and Seb were in their own race up front, but I had my eye on the McLarens. Fortunately, Rubens was quick enough with me in tow, and I managed to jump both Lewis and Jenson when they pitted mid-race. But then, as so often happens at street circuits, there was more drama: Kobayashi nosed the wall at Turn 18, collected Bruno Senna's Hispania and the safety car came out for the second time. A spot on the podium was now mine for the taking ...

Whichever way you look at it, the night belonged to Ferrari and Fernando.

When racing resumed on lap 36, I thought, 'This is going to be interesting: I've got the two Virgins to clear but Lewis has the speed on me.' Brazilian Lucas di Grassi in the number 25 car caused me the most problems. I was going to have a look at Turn 5 but he didn't give me the line – he was hard to follow and it was tricky getting on the power to muster enough exit speed. This presented Lewis with an opportunity – he was the hunter in this chase – and his racing instincts told him he could have a crack. He tried to get by me on the outside through Turn 7 – the left-hander – but I held my line. Suddenly we touched and he came out of it worse for wear, suffering a puncture to his left rear tyre. It was another unfortunate racing incident – no one was to blame – and the stewards agreed (no doubt with input from the weekend's 'guest' official, former F1 and Indy Car driver, Danny Sullivan).

For the remainder of the race I had massive vibration through the steering: the collision had dislodged the tyre from the front right wheel and the beading was the only thing keeping it together! It was a concern, having done all the hard work throughout the race, but it went the distance. With Lewis out and Jenson unable to apply any pressure, I came home in third, claiming my first

ever podium in the Lion City. Crucially, the 15 points I earned meant that I still led the Drivers' Championship. Seb finished second, putting him into fourth overall and just one point behind Lewis, who was now 20 points adrift of me after two straight DNFs.

But it was clear the enemy no longer wore red and white – he just wore red. Fernando Alonso won the first Singapore Grand Prix in 2008 and was on the podium again in 2009. He's always quick around Marina Bay; but even he doesn't quite know why! In 2010 he took pole, punched in the fastest lap of the race and claimed victory – which made two in a row, back-to-back with Monza. The gap between us in the Drivers' Championship had narrowed to 11 points; Suzuka was going to be very interesting indeed ...

Marina Bay has always been a bit of a puzzle ...

This time I was beginning to see the light!

JAPAN

Pole Position:
Sebastian Vettel (RBR–Renault),
1:30.785 = 230.271 km/h
[MW front row, 1:30.853]

Fastest Lap:
Mark Webber (RBR–Renault),
1:33.474 = 223.647 km/h, lap 53

Podium:
1. Sebastian Vettel (RBR–Renault)
2. Mark Webber (RBR–Renault)
3. Fernando Alonso (Ferrari)

Drivers' World Championship:
1. Webber 220 points
2. Alonso 206
3. Vettel 206

Constructors' World Championship:
1. RBR–Renault 426 points
2. McLaren–Mercedes 381
3. Ferrari 334

JAPAN
FORMATION FINISH

The sun shone in the end – but
it was a long time coming!

RACE 16 >>> SUZUKA

Race Date: 10 October 2010
Circuit Name: Suzuka
Number of Laps: 53
Circuit Length: 5.807 km
Race Distance: 307.471 km
Lap Record: 1:31.540 – K Räikkönen (2005)

FORMATION FINISH

If I thought heading home to Australia ahead of Japan might make life easier, I had another think coming. On the Sunday morning before Suzuka, I got on a mountain bike for the first time since my accident in Tasmania at the end of 2008. I was riding with a great mate of mine. Suddenly, he crashed right in front of me and I had nowhere to go but straight between the ears of the horse! I suffered what they call a skier's fracture to my right shoulder. Suzuka is a brutal track, so it was a blessing that the Japanese weather gave me an enforced rest day on the Saturday, and a pre-race injection helped, too. In the end we got through the weekend all right – but 3.8 metres was to come between me and my fifth Grand Prix victory of the season.

The Japanese Grand Prix is traditionally one of the last, if not the last race of the season, and over the past 24 years, ten World Champions have been decided there. We went into the race knowing it was a track where the RB6 should work really well, especially through the sinuous first sector. In fact, looking over the final four venues of the season, we felt we shouldn't have any weak ones. We only knew the Korean track in theory of course, since this year was the inaugural race.

So I headed for Ino, Suzuka City, knowing how helpful it would be if I could win another race to put some more distance between me and the other guys in the title fight. At the same

No accounting for taste ...

Heikki Kovalainen's crew gave him a special lid in honour of his heroics in Singapore ...

time, consistency is so important in this business and that's what we had to aim for, too.

Although the first free practice session was dry, Lewis still managed to get into trouble, crashing out at the notorious right-hand Degner curve. The third practice session was washed out due to heavy storms, which hadn't abated by Saturday. It isn't the first time we've had to do qualifying and the race on the same day: back in 2004 all running on Saturday was cancelled due to Typhoon Ma-on. This year, I did just one installation lap on Saturday before we all thought better of it. When F1 crews are spending more time building model boats and floating them down pit lane than actually getting cars ready for

No chance
of any spot
fires in these
conditions.

quick laps you know you don't want to be out there driving! From then on it all reminded me of testing – doing nothing for a whole day. Maybe not being allowed to test during the season any more has its upside!

On Sunday the track dried up enough for qualifying, but I missed out on pole by six one-hundredths of a second. Our RB6 was completing a lap of Suzuka at an average of 230 kilometres an hour, so on a circuit where it's so difficult to overtake, that six one-hundredths of a second – which translates to about 3.8 metres – made all the difference. Don't get me wrong: I know the gap between Seb and me in Sunday's race was wider than that in the end. But on Sunday morning, my teammate had that extra half-tenth on me and it gave him track position in the race.

This was another weekend where some of my challengers came a cropper. After Lewis had that fairly heavy 'off' on Friday, McLaren had to fly in some parts for his car, and he was penalised five grid spots for changing his gearbox. But that was nothing compared to what happened in the race itself. Before we even got to the starting grid, Lucas di Grassi fishtailed off the track near the entrance to the notorious 130R turn. After the marshals cleared di Grassi's Virgin, we got off the start, but there was more drama to come. I'm glad I was safely on the front row ahead of all the action as I don't think I've ever seen anything quite like it! First the Russian driver Vitaly Petrov's Renault collected Nico Hulkenberg's Williams, taking them both out; then just a few metres later Felipe's Ferrari went hurtling across the track and collected Vitantonio Liuzzi in the Force India, so they

Maybe Michael was praying for rain because he is always brilliant in the wet!

were both gone, too. I thought that Felipe might pop up in the remaining races and give Fernando a helping hand, but it clearly wasn't going to happen in Japan.

Meanwhile I was having some problems of my own. Robert Kubica's Renault left the line like a rocket and got in between me and Seb, which was not the start I had been looking for, and getting past a car that quick in a straight line would have been no gimme. But then as we went around behind the safety car he suddenly slowed – he was missing his right rear wheel! It's no boast to say that from the time the safety car went back in, there was never any question about the result. If I had little real chance of getting past Seb unless he made a mistake, then Fernando behind us and the others behind him (the two McLarens included) were never in a position to challenge Red Bull for the win. As I said at the time, it was a formation finish for us from about lap 9 onwards. There was a moment near the end when Webber fans might have been a little nervous as Fernando's Ferrari closed the gap, but I had him covered the whole time.

If I couldn't get the win, I could at least have some fun – and I did that on the final lap. Seb and I had been trading fastest times for much of the race and on the very last time round I made sure I finished up with the fastest lap of the race. Couldn't let my teammate get away with what we call the 'triple crown' of pole, race win and fastest lap, could I? It was especially nice to have the man who designed the RB6, Adrian Newey, up there on the podium with us. It was the first time he had been to Japan in a decade and I felt it was appropriate he should be there.

Suzuka had proved something I already knew: the RB6 was the best racing car I had ever driven. With Lewis and JB behind us, the result meant that Fernando and Seb were now tied for second, with Fernando technically ahead on race wins. But my margin had widened by three points to 14 with three races to go. And of course it was the best possible result for us in the Constructors' Championship, with that gap now out to 45 points over McLaren.

Next up: Korea. It's always fun to go to a new track, even though this one had been the subject of will-it-or-won't-it-be-ready controversy for much of the year. A few laps would be all it would take to learn the new layout, then it'd be business as usual – and any of the top five drivers could win.

There's rain, and then there's what hit us on Saturday in Japan.

The start was chaotic: Petrov's Renault was going nowhere ...

Liuzzi was in a bad state after he collided with Massa.

181

**Robert Kubica
made a rocket
start but the
Renault didn't
last long.**

JAPANESE GRAND PRIX

SUZUKA 2010

Seb's pointing out that this place belongs to us!

Whatever floats your boat – at least we didn't meet the *Titanic*'s fate!

KOREA
IT NEVER RAINS
BUT IT POURS

KOREA

Red truck, no Bull
– and practically no
car after my shunt.

Race Date:	24 October 2010
Circuit Name:	Korea International Circuit
Number of Laps:	55
Circuit Length:	5.621 km
Race Distance:	309.155 km
Lap Record:	1:50.257 – F Alonso (2010)

IT NEVER RAINS BUT IT POURS

So much had been said in the media and around the paddock about the new South Korean venue – Would it be ready? Would we be going? Would it be cancelled? – that it was a relief in the end to get there and get on with it. Lewis, Jenson, Heikki, Nico Rosberg and I hired a private plane out of Tokyo to take us to a little airport just 45 minutes from the Yeongam track. It worked out well, because the track is in a remote province, about 400 kilometres south of Seoul, a city I still haven't been to.

Straight away it was obvious the new venue was very raw. There was so much work still to be done in the 48 hours leading up to the race that they had to get the army in! It should all develop nicely over the next few years, though, with plans for a city and a marina to be built around the track. Everyone was friendly enough, and the facilities for the teams were pretty good. The organisers did really well with the crowd – a fact which only hit home when we came to leave on Sunday.

Part of the development will be getting the track itself bedded in. It was pretty dusty to begin with, as I found out in one little spinning moment on Friday, but from a driving perspective it's unique.

We were still five. This shot recalled the famous 'Gang of Four' photo from Adelaide in 1986 featuring title contenders Nigel Mansell, Nelson Piquet, Ayrton Senna and Alain Prost.

It was designed by the German architect Hermann Tilke (the guy behind the Sepang, Shanghai and Abu Dhabi tracks, among others) and it has a bit of everything. Part of the circuit is permanent and part of it is temporary, built just for the F1 race. There are some quick corners but overall it's not mega-fast. It starts with two long straights, but it's also got technical stuff that begins at turns 10 and 11 and goes on from there like a street circuit. It's a good little lap.

We landed in the middle of a media frenzy of calculations about title chances, speculation over team orders, and so on. All I knew was that the Spanish were probably having a ball, with Fernando closing in as Seb and I continued to fight it

out. I had to keep doing what I'd been doing – finishing races and accumulating points. Again qualifying was very, very close. A few times this year Seb and I have exchanged settings on the RB6 and this time he used mine after a low-key Friday. On Saturday afternoon we had a fantastic fight: it was nip and tuck throughout qualifying between the two of us. Seb went fastest in Q1, I was on top in Q2 and, finally, Seb took pole by just 0.074 of a second. Some expressed surprise that I opted to do two timed laps on my final run, but I felt more comfortable doing it that way and I was happy with my lap. Sometimes your lap time can come down to something as unpredictable as the amount of wind you run into on the

All eyes on you-know-who as the title chasers face the press.

Of course I was happy to lend a hand ...

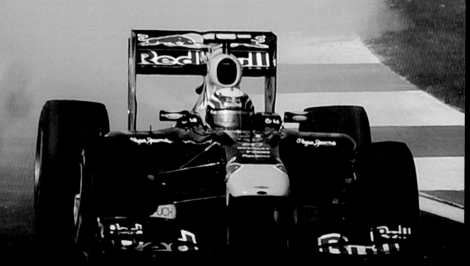

The early signs were that dust, not water, would be the problem.

straight, but however you look at it, Seb deserved pole.

I'd said on Friday that everybody was in the same boat – but I didn't mean for the local weather to take it literally! The forecast for Sunday was for rain only in the morning, and to be honest I was glad to see it. I knew the rain would clean up the asphalt on the dirty side of the track – where I was starting – and that might level the playing field a bit. It didn't look that bad on the formation lap, and I actually felt starting behind the safety car was a bit over the top ...

But the first lap changed all that.

The going was tough with visibility severely reduced and I thought, 'Jesus Christ! How bad's this?' There were no actual 'rivers', but because the track was new and unused (not even a support race had been around it), under the downpour there was now a film of one or two millimetres of water sitting perfectly on top of the asphalt.

There were messages coming in over the radio from most of the drivers about the weather. I gather Fernando, who was third on the grid, said that these were the worst conditions he had ever driven in and that he couldn't see me in front of him. The race was red-flagged after three laps, so we had another long interruption before getting under way, again behind the safety car, at five past four local time. After 17 laps, safety car driver Bernd Mayländer brought the safety car in which I thought was a reasonable call, and we were finally going racing.

Come qualifying, Seb was the blue-eyed boy again – but by yet another bee's dick.

I felt pretty good at the restart and was just sitting with Seb for the first few corners, trying to get into a rhythm. The first time racing through Turn 12, I went wide, trying a wider line to see if there was better grip out there. But I didn't go too wide and I thought it was a low-risk thing to do. But next lap at the same spot I got behind the kerb, lost the rear of the car, then got on the white line and once that happened, it was all over. It was totally my fault. Not only that, as I spun I ruined

Once again rain stopped play –
for quite a while, at least.

Top three on the road, top three in the title chase – at least in the early Korean running ...

An early exit meant a ride back to the pits.

Nico Rosberg's race, too, as his Mercedes simply couldn't avoid me on the way through.

It'd be nice to be able to push a rewind button, but these things happen in motor racing. It's just that some days they hurt more than others. This year we've had a lot of amazing highs and not too many lows, and people forget that Fernando hit a white line in Spa and copped the same result. It was a day when things just didn't work out for me. Or for the team, as it happened, because Seb's engine blew up spectacularly when he seemed to be cruising to the win.

So Fernando left Korea 11 points to the good with me out of the lead for the first time in six races. But there would have been 60 times in a racing year when you go

He may wear his hat the wrong way, but Nico Rosberg was doing everything right and it was a shame I took him out with me.

It never rains ... Seb over-stressed his engine and our bad day was complete.

through micro-moments like that and they go undetected, and I came away believing I could still win the title.

Mind you, I came away slowly in the sea of traffic. The race finished very late and our private plane was due to take off at 8 pm. All five of us left the track, amazingly enough, in separate cars, but only Lewis and I made it there on time, and at that point Lewis bailed. I tried to get the flight going, but Narita International Airport in Japan shuts at 11 pm and we wouldn't have made it. I was walking out of the airport when I bumped into Lotus boss Tony Fernandes, who was heading to Kuala Lumpur, so I hitched a lift with him, had four hours in the airport there and caught a Malaysian Airlines flight home.

Next stop: Brazil. We would go there with loads of positives: I'd been so close to pole in the last two races; I'd put in a very good drive in Japan ... and Brazil's a track I know my way around. Who knew how Fernando would go, or even if he might get some help from his Brazilian teammate? As for the team orders, Seb was now fourth behind Lewis and 14 points adrift of me still in second spot. But the damage had been done; I was out of the lead. The writing had been on the wall for Red Bull earlier in the season, and now we were continuing to make it hard on ourselves by not favouring one driver over the other. Not a lot had changed between Seb and me, but what had changed was that some other bloke had got out in front of us. Whichever way you skin it, we were all on the points we were on ...

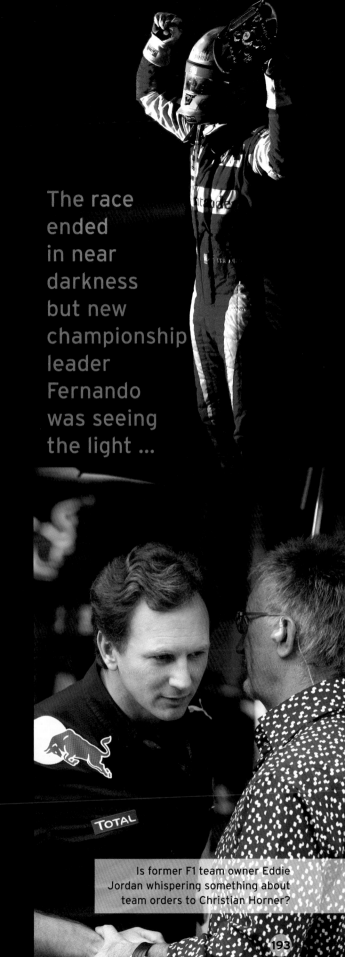

The race ended in near darkness but new championship leader Fernando was seeing the light ...

Is former F1 team owner Eddie Jordan whispering something about team orders to Christian Horner?

BRAZIL

A SENSATIONAL DAY

BRAZIL

Pole Position:
Nico Hulkenberg (Williams–Cosworth),
1:14.470 = 208.304 km/h
[MW P3, 1:15.637]

Fastest Lap:
Lewis Hamilton (McLaren–Mercedes),
1:13.851 = 210.049 km/h, lap 66
[MW: 1:14.047, lap 69]

Podium:
1. Sebastian Vettel (RBR–Renault)
2. Mark Webber (RBR–Renault)
3. Fernando Alonso (Ferrari)

Drivers' World Championship:
1. Alonso 246 points
2. Webber 238
3. Vettel 231

Constructors' World Championship:
1. RBR–Renault 469 points
2. McLaren–Mercedes 421
3. Ferrari 389

RACE 18 >>> SÃO PAULO

Race Date: 7 November 2010
Circuit Name: Autódromo José Carlos Pace (Interlagos)
Number of Laps: 71
Circuit Length: 4.309 km
Race Distance: 305.909 km
Lap Record: 1:11.473 – JP Montoya (2004)

A SENSATIONAL DAY

The Korean disaster left everyone at Red Bull Racing feeling just a little less comfortable than before. We could have won the Constructors' Championship there, but instead we hadn't scored a single point. That uneasiness only worsened once we got to São Paulo on Brazil's south coast.

There is still a part of me that likes a bit of controversy to fire myself up; it's hard to be a goody two-shoes all the time when you're in such a political sport. People want you to play with a straight bat and express your feelings, so that's exactly what I did when asked if there had been equal treatment for Seb and me within Red Bull Racing. I said technically, that was the case,

but emotionally, well, it was obvious where the team's sympathies lay. I'm not stupid, I know what's going on, that's how it is, and I said so.

Some days are just quiet news days, I suppose, and that's why my remarks got such an airing. The British media ran wild with it. The thing that disappointed me most was that some of the Red Bull Racing workforce thought my remarks were angled at them, which of course they weren't. Fortunately, there was to be some happier news for them a couple of days later ...

Qualifying at Interlagos was brutal – one of the toughest of the year – with rain, a greasy track, a drying line, then wet conditions again. It's easy to get things

The city has its good and bad sides, but Interlagos is a great place to race.

wrong in conditions like that. In the wet we were quick – I was fastest in both Q1 and Q2 – but what became blatantly obvious was that we had some enormous decisions to make at incredibly short notice. We didn't know how the slick tyres were going to take to the track, and whatever choice we made was going to be a big gamble. So everyone went out, put their best foot forward and laid down a banker on the intermediate tyres. But as the track started to dry out, it became clear that if you stayed on the intermediates for the next six or seven minutes, pretty soon it was going to be the wrong tyre.

I think a lot of calls were made from the cockpits – I did my time on the intermediates and then rang Ciaron to say I was coming in for slicks. Lewis dived into the pits in front of me, which was a good sign, and then Seb came in, too, so the main contenders were all thinking in a similar way. But now I was snookered: Felipe wasn't massively comfortable ahead of me on his slicks and I had Seb behind me, so I ended up the meat in the sandwich.

I finished my first lap quite close to Felipe, which didn't help my concentration. I kept thinking, 'Should I bail out of this one? How close is Seb?' The first time I came down the hill completely hot, it was still a lot damper than we thought. I went off the track – nothing major – but it made for a pretty ropey opening to the next lap.

It was a tense weekend – but there's always time for a laugh with Ciaron.

Meeting the kids was a nice way to ease some of the strain of the second-last race of the year.

It was bloody tight for everyone – everyone except Nico Hulkenberg, that is! Cast your mind back to Monza and you'll remember how frustrated I was by the rookie driver's on-track behaviour. Well, here he was in Brazil nabbing his first F1 pole position. No complaints this time; in fact, he did a great lap – it was as though he was driving on a different racetrack. I was happy to get third when I could easily have got 17th. In a way, qualifying was a bullet dodged. The top guys were all there – and the pressure was on again.

For the race, we were pretty confident we had Nico covered because in the dry the Williams wasn't particularly competitive. So it was good to see that Lewis and especially Fernando were behind the Red Bulls in

Nico Hulkenberg made us all look pretty second-rate in qualifying – and you can tell what Seb and I thought of that!

2010 FORMULA 1 GRANDE PRÊMIO PETROBRAS DO BRASIL

Not that there was much attention on us in Brazil ...

Seb got past Nico into Turn 1;
I had to wait just a little bit longer.

Jenson got stung in qualifying, though
he fought back well to be fifth – but
Brazil, where he won the title last year,
was also where he lost it this year.

fourth and fifth spots on the grid. Jenson – the last member of the so-called 'Famous Five' the photographers had made such a fuss of in Korea – didn't make it through to Q3, so qualifying could hardly have worked out better for us.

On Sunday, the weather held and when the lights finally went out I had a good opening lap. I knew it was critical to line Nico up in the first sector, and with the wind blowing in a different direction from our last dry running on Friday, I felt the run down to Turn 4 was the spot to overtake him. I knew I wasn't going to be able to get in as deep on brakes so I left a margin, but he tried to brake later and ran wide.

Jenson wasn't able to help Lewis all that much – and Felipe had a rotten weekend in his home race as well.

I then followed Seb, who managed to pull out a two-second lead and stayed like that for ages. At about lap 30, the team noticed a problem with my engine, but they didn't tell me until I'd done nearly 40 laps. We were going to have to change our pattern – higher gears for some corners and short-shifting to give the engine a bit of a breather. The car responded okay but

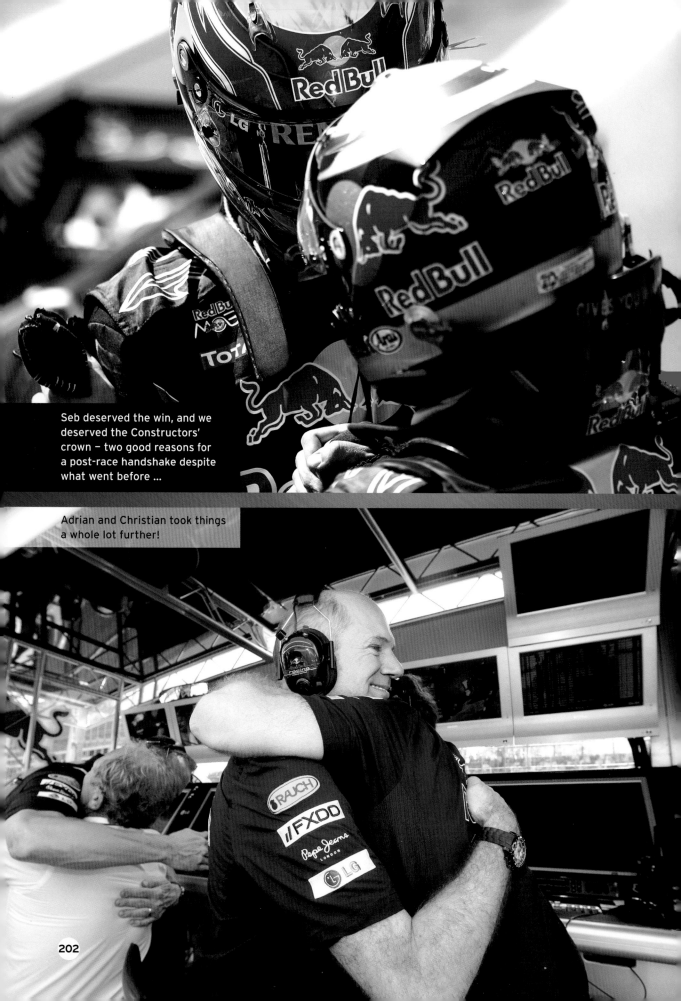

Seb deserved the win, and we deserved the Constructors' crown – two good reasons for a post-race handshake despite what went before ...

Adrian and Christian took things a whole lot further!

the guys were still nervous. Luckily for me, a safety car was deployed when Vitantonio Liuzzi crashed his Force India into the wall exiting Turn 2 – but the safety car wasn't out for long. The race was over in terms of challenging Seb; now my focus was on Fernando and getting the engine home for that second place – because the title race would have been all over if I hadn't.

When Seb and I shook hands in the paddock, it was basically because we knew we had sealed the Constructors' title for the team. That was a special moment for lots of different reasons. I thought immediately of people like my former teammate David Coulthard, who'd had a big influence on the team, and others who'd worked hard for Red Bull Racing over many years. It's not

only what we did that weekend that won us the title: it takes a long time. I've been part of that as well, as have Adrian and so many unsung heroes who have been there the whole way through.

So after a really tough weekend in Korea, winning the Constructors' Championship with a dominant one–two finish in Brazil made for a sensational day. The team had put everything into our cars this year and we'd won, and that was a huge achievement. Could we win a second title – the one I really wanted – a week later in Abu Dhabi?

It would be us versus him in Abu Dhabi. Maybe that's the message I was trying to get across to Fernando.

I don't think that's the animal the team was named after, somehow!

One down, one to go ...

203

UNITED ARAB EMIRATES

A SMALL HOLE

ABU DHABI

Pole Position:
Sebastian Vettel (RBR–Renault),
1:39.394 = 201.163 km/h
[MW P5, 1:39.925]

Fastest Lap:
Lewis Hamilton (McLaren–Mercedes),
1:41.274 = 197.428 km/h, lap 47
[MW: 1:42.196, lap 52]

Podium:
1. Sebastian Vettel (RBR–Renault)
2. Lewis Hamilton (McLaren–Mercedes)
3. Jenson Button (McLaren–Mercedes)
[MW P8]

Drivers' World Championship:
1. Vettel 256 points
2. Alonso 252
3. Webber 242

Constructors' World Championship:
1. RBR–Renault 498 points
2. McLaren–Mercedes 454
3. Ferrari 396

RACE 19 >>> ABU DHABI

Race Date:	14 November 2010
Circuit Name:	Yas Marina Circuit
Number of Laps:	55
Circuit Length:	5.554 km
Race Distance:	305.355 km
Lap Record:	1:40.279 – S Vettel (2009)

A SMALL HOLE

The distance from Bahrain to Abu Dhabi, as the crow flies, is about 425 kilometres. As the Formula 1 circus travels the globe, the distance from the first race at Sakhir to the last at Yas Marina is many thousands of kilometres and more than 1100 racing laps. For me in 2010, it was a journey from what some people thought was number two driver status to genuine World Championship contender.

You would have got pretty good odds on me at the start of the year, but by the time we reached the spectacular circuit on Abu Dhabi's Yas Island those odds had shortened considerably. Fernando, with eight points in hand over me and 15 over Seb, was obviously in the strongest position of us all, but Lewis was an outside chance, too. His McLaren had been impressively quick in Brazil and the two long straights in Abu Dhabi meant the Red Bulls might struggle for outright speed.

I certainly struggled in qualifying, and still can't quite figure out why. I was in the top four throughout the practice sessions, and on Saturday afternoon I was pretty happy with my performance in Q1 and Q2. I was in the hunt – doing similar times to the McLarens and a tenth or two off Seb – but come Q3, I didn't go with the track and just couldn't squeeze a decent time out of the tyres. When I saw the target on the pit board I felt I just couldn't get there. Normally you can react to whatever's on the board, but not this time. It was a difficult five minutes for

The usual end-of-season photo was hot work …

Especially as this bloke was giving us curry!

The last few minutes of qualifying were fraught.

The top three in qualifying: spot the missing Australian.

me to get the pace, and dropping to fifth on the grid was far from ideal.

At the season opener in Bahrain, I realised almost as soon as I went out how vital qualifying was going to be within the new F1 rules, and the 19th race only underlined that painful fact. There were so many possible permutations of results and points it made your head spin, but it was obvious that not starting on the front row was going to be a major handicap. We'll have to make sure we're there more often next year.

The 2010 Abu Dhabi Grand Prix had barely begun when we had a safety car after Michael spun early in the opening lap. Vitantonio Liuzzi had absolutely nowhere to go and went over the top of him. It looked

Michael's comeback season ended in a harsh way.

like a big accident at the time but they were both out of their cars quickly and apparently unharmed – unlike my title chances. I didn't have mega-grip in the first stint with the rear tyres, so we thought we'd roll the dice on our race strategy and pit on lap 12 to change to the harder compound. A few drivers had already pitted while the safety car was out – but I wasn't made aware of that and unfortunately couldn't clear them in our stop. That was the checkmate, really.

Ironically, this all helped Seb. When I pitted, Ferrari and Fernando felt they had to cover us off, so Fernando came in three laps after me. On the first two laps after I rejoined the race, I lost a lot of time behind Jaime Alguersuari and couldn't take on Fernando when he rejoined ahead of me.

Once I stopped, Ferrari brought Fernando in to cover me.

Unfortunately, although Abu Dhabi is a spectacular place, there are few chances to pass ...

Then he got trapped battling with Vitaly Petrov's Renault, which has the same engine as ours. Petrov was very difficult to overtake because he had good top speed, but he wasn't so good in the corners. Even so, Fernando couldn't find a way past him and I was stuck behind them both. That was the key to the race; it was a stalemate after that as far as I was concerned.

Congratulations must go to Seb on winning the Drivers' Championship. In the end he led it at the right race – the last one. The other four of us led at different stages – and I led for a long stretch in the middle of the season – but Seb drove a great race in Abu Dhabi and it earned him the title of youngest World Champion in the history of our sport.

That, and finishing eighth, left me feeling pretty empty on Sunday night. We had a chance to do something incredible and unique but in the end it didn't turn out for us. It's always tough when you come so close but miss out in the final stages, but we were certainly in the hunt for much of the season. I refuse to look at 2010 as anything other than a year full of positives. As I said at the press conference that kick-started the final weekend, if I didn't win the title there was obviously going to be a small hole, but I feel I drove very well for most of the season, and that's the most important thing to me.

I've got a lot of respect for the guys I race against and that's why you get out of bed – to try and beat them. But in this game you focus on your own performance and you do your very best in order to get the job done. When I started in F1 I didn't have a winning car, but in 2009 and 2010 I showed what I was capable of if I had the right machinery. Four race wins, including two of the blue riband events, Monaco and Silverstone, which every driver wants to have in his trophy cabinet; five pole positions; three fastest race laps; and 10 podiums – it was a hell of a season and one I'll always be proud of.

And there's always next year ...

Hats off to Seb: he got
the timing just right.

Sometimes you walk
away empty-handed ...

You just have to put your best foot forward next time.

Wardrobe malfunction – the weekend started and finished badly!

2010 FORMULA 1 ETIHAD AIRWAYS ABU DHABI GRAND PR

ACKNOWLEDGEMENTS

My sincere thanks to all 550 staff at Red Bull Racing and Red Bull Technology for making 2010 my best season yet.

Extra special thanks to Christian Horner, Adrian Newey, Peter Prodromou, Rob Marshall, Mark Ellis, Ian Morgan, Paul Monaghan, Paul Everington, Jonathan Wheatley, Will Courtenay, Terry Brice, Matt Cadieux, Chris Charnley, Paul Field, Neil Waterman, Ciaron Pilbeam, Dan Ferrey, Gavin Ward, Tim White, Kenny Handkammer, Jayne Poole, Dominik Mitsch, Katie Tweedle, Nicole Carling, Thelma Spragg, all the boys who bolted together my RB5s and RB6s – you know who you are and what you mean to me – and to Christian Kolleritsch and his tireless Red Bull hospitality crew.

Thanks to the team at Renault at Viry-Chatillon with whom I've enjoyed a long association, to Kerry Fenwick and Paulene Saunders for running a tight ship back at base, Dave Aldridge for running my supporters club, the club members for their patience and sticking by me, the locals at The Stag, Mentmore, for their support, to Stuart Sykes for making sense of my words and turning them into something I hope you've enjoyed reading, and to Pan Macmillan for bringing them to life.

Thanks to my great family and close circle of friends for sharing the journey thus far, and to those who patched me up after my accident in Tasmania and got me back in the cockpit, in particular Roger Cleary, David Hahn and Eva Sobonova; to Simon Sostaric for his contribution this season, and last but not least to Dietrich Mateschitz and the Yoovidhya family for giving me wings.

MARK WEBBER

PICTURE CREDITS